The Resting Place

A Graveside Diary
By Pamela Little

Paul and Susan,

Thank you for making your airbnb home a resting place away from our family drama!

Pamela

Memorial Day 2015

SOUL CUSTODY PRESS • REDLANDS, CA

....

Published by

SOUL CUSTODY PRESS

Redlands, CA

....

Book and cover design by Jenny VanSeters, Santa Barbara, CA
Printed in the United States of America

....

ISBN-13 978-0-9907848-0-7
Library of Congress Control Number: 2014916806

....

To those in search of a resting place

....

Preface

This is my journal, which I titled *The Resting Place*. It was written from May 24, 2010, to April 28, 2014. Because it is a diary, there are two considerations to keep in mind as you read:

(1) What I've written may reflect only the day and time of the writing, which means

(2) it may have been true in that particular moment but is no longer valid.

Why should you read my diary? Because it is a testimony to the power of journal keeping to capture real time and shape its course. Diaries reflect immediate time in that our words are only meant for the moment we write them and are out of context the next. They're about process, not permanence, which is why journaling is so cathartic and healing. Our words move us down the blank pages of our lives.

Hopefully, this journal will reflect to you the power behind the paper as the pen kept pushing me forward.

Now that I've written this disclaimer, you have permission to read my diary. I hope it inspires you to write yours.

Pamela Lee Little

Introduction

On August 7, 2009, at the age of forty-three, I bought my plot at Gateway Memorial Park in Southern California. Grand total: $10,518.30. With payments of $120.43 for eighty-four months, I wondered how I could make use of the investment now, while I'm still alive. What if I could use it like a backyard? Just stop by now and then to hang out. It would be like a gym membership, only I'd exercise my spiritual fitness. Whenever I need a resting place, I could visit the final one in advance. It could be a near-death experience without a crisis.

Those plot visits developed into a graveside writing ritual. I didn't know ahead of time what I would write. I only knew that whatever transpired, it had to come from The Resting Place. As I sank into the pages, I discovered myself buried alive. Like the sun rising on the cemetery, I left The Resting Place resurrected.

There is a specific way I write that happens only in this place. Certain words are reserved for The Resting Place alone, like comments spoken about someone at a memorial service. But in this case, the words are said before the end.

The plot thickens ...

Flash Forward

AUGUST 21, 2073
Interred, Gateway Memorial Park

Hello. I'm writing to you from beyond the grave, a diary entry from the future as an experiment to introduce a book written sixty years ago. (I kind of figured I'd be dead by age 106.)

Life from this perspective is quite shallow. A few ashes inside an urn tucked into the earth underneath this stone. The view's pretty limited. I can't move. Or breathe. Or talk. It's quiet here most days. I wish they'd turn that fake fountain off, though. And that people would stop adding stuff to it to make bubbles. It looks like a hot tub in prank mode. Tacky.

Look, I don't have much to say. You're lucky you're alive. Death is way overrated.

Day One

MAY 24, 2010
Graveside, Gateway Memorial Park

Finally! I'm at my final resting place. First time I've come since I bought the place nine months ago. I would like to know who my next door neighbor is, the woman whose name is on the plaque in front of me, which says she took up residence in 2004.

It's too cold by my deathbed, except for the sight of the sunlit roses. I won't notice the temperature when I'm in the ground. They call it a resting place. Well, I'm using it while alive.

Seven Months Later

JANUARY 8, 2011
Graveside, Gateway Memorial Park

My mother doesn't care where we put her. When I asked, she seemed to think I was trying to hurry it up for the money. Actually, I was trying to spare myself the added grief of guesswork when the time comes. But now I'm thinking the urn next to me, which I thought would be for a future spouse, will really be for my mom. Yes. This area of Gateway's garden district is perfect for her service, as well.

It bothers me that I don't know who the woman is in the grave next to mine. A young forty-eight at death. My neighbor for the rest of my life, and no one in my life will know her either. I feel obligated to introduce her now to the people who will be visiting me here one day.

An acquaintance from a self-help program for people with money issues knows that I'm writing from my plot here, and she thinks it's a good marketing idea for the cemetery. "You have to publish this somehow," she said. Right. Like every other book idea I've had. Besides, this is too personal. She said she was going to do the same thing … find a final resting place and go there now. She says the purchase is secured debt because I can sell this spot. It's a salable asset. But until death do us not part, because now that I've grown accustomed to it, it's like a home to me.

I'm tired of thinking that every new idea I have is a book. To approach my resting place as if it is a groundbreaker goes against everything it stands for. It means that my life is marketable or of interest to others. Up for grabs. It isn't. At times, my life is of no interest even to me. After all, how freely have I given my life away to the path of self-destruction?

Do we all at times try to destroy ourselves? One good way to accomplish that is to do it slowly by overeating. Nobody notices. Eventually, they see the fat but not the death wish. If you eat enough sugar in low doses over time, it might disguise itself as some seemingly unrelated condition. Even when traced back to poor diet, all is forgiven, because we're all human and we all like to eat. We have to eat.

Death of the spirit is far more fatal than death of the body, and body and spirit feel equally crushed after a divorce. I call it Post-Divorce Destruction Disorder, PDDD. No, there isn't a pill for it yet that I'm aware of. It is characterized by rapid weight loss in the initial radioactive phase of divorcing, perhaps coinciding with a rebound relationship, and leads to weight gain due to fierce attempts to bury grief and anger, while at the same time warding off the opposite sex in case that doesn't work out either.

After my divorce, I had a dream that I was comatose in a field of Hershey Bars and my mother and my children's father had to haul me off to the psych ward. Yesterday, I purposely ate a Hershey Bar after not having one in twelve years. When the binge followed, I realized the dream had transpired. Only I hauled myself off to The Resting Place to get a grip before going into a sugar coma. For some reason, I woke this morning with a ferocious desire to write, similar to my ferocious desire to eat yesterday. My spirit was reborn overnight, needing to coexist with the temptation that death is a bite away. It's far more likely my physical death from overeating will take a lot longer than this instantaneous spirit death. So I'll take my reborn spirit in my 140-pound body, which could reach 240 or 340 one day. I don't want my cup in the ground filled with ashes to overfloweth.

Today I visited Phyllis, my ninety-two-year-old godmother, for what felt like the last time. During a run on frozen yogurt, midstream on a binge. She was busy designating items in the house to family members, recording them on paper. She asked me if there was anything I wanted dibs on in the house. It made me wonder if she had any Dibs® in the refrigerator, those ice cream balls they serve in movie theaters. I couldn't think of one sentimental object. Even the drawing of the "om" universal sound she showed me seemed so irrelevant in light of my freezer worship. Because of this overriding preoccupation with food, I felt no loss of Phyllis, no pain from the business-gone-south with me and her son, no sadness, no attachment to those possessions representing her entire life.

She just looked at me. Because I've known her for seventeen years, I could tell she sensed something wasn't right with me, and her quizzical gaze snapped me out of my spell. *Phyllis, your journals!* I really wanted the writing of her life behind the newspaper column she wrote. But she was talking about dibs on items, and those journals were off limits. In fact, she's already destroyed most of them in preparation for what she does want to leave behind. Finally, I replied. "Any journals remaining that you didn't destroy and don't leave with your family, I'm happy to have."

Anyway, today I am here to choose life. This is my new start date for abstinence from compulsive overeating. Day One. It's that easy to decide, since the Hershey field is at hand. I always wondered what that dream meant, because it seemed like such a foreshadowing. Just like the recurring dream of the car explosion in which I die alone. Recently, I contemplated selling my car and getting a bicycle. When overeating, I am a dangerous, speedy, careless driver, and I always ate while driving in binge mode. Drive-throughs enable a quick getaway and multiple runs through endless locations without being suspected for volume or repetition. Because of these driving premonitions, I shouldn't even be in a car. So I think I will sell it. I don't need it. Can I avert death by car explosion by never getting into a car? Yes. Chances are, you can't die in a car if you don't drive or get into one. Life and grocery shopping will be much harder without a car. So will a full-time job requiring a commute. What about picking up the kids after school? Averting death is so inconvenient.

I made a big mistake and called Mom with the news that I had found my final resting place. Though treated, I was still in a manic phase of bipolar disorder, when the alpha and omega come together in cosmic conversation (usually a one-way conversation, since in that mode I am the cosmos). Word to the wise. Don't call Mom and act all happy about death. That's the other phone call parents dread most. Her response to my elation about securing my spot for the hereafter was "How odd, Pamela. Is there something you're not telling me?" And you know how it goes. The only word I heard was "odd." So I missed her genuine concern and, instead, took it upon myself to dive into the inordinate shame most manic depressives eventually feel, which proceeds to snap us out of the spell of the day.

Five Months Later

JUNE 10, 2011
Graveside, Gateway Memorial Park

The plot is paid off. Can you believe it? Somehow the topic of my plot came up again when my mom considered a move to Redlands from La Jolla and then decided against it. I had told her I wanted to be with her in the final years, not specifying hers or mine, and I asked Mom to "move in." I explained that she would become the other page in the open-book design I've chosen for the marker. That's when she said she'd pay for the rest of it but leave it in my name.

I'm glad I have a stake in it; she never lets me pay for anything for her. But this, yes. Perhaps she is happy letting me pay some portion of it so she won't have to check out while thinking no one else did their part, while she spent her entire life supporting her children. Now that the plot is paid off, I want Mom to see it but don't know how to get her here from La Jolla. I'd have to come up with some other reason for the visit and then say, "Hey, let's drive by our final resting place." But I'm afraid she would notice my excitement and once more misconstrue it as eagerness for her money. I feel sad she may never see it beforehand.

I should have brought her here on a recent visit. But she's so full of life that the thought of death never occurs to me when I'm around her. My mother is immortal to me, and her health is evidence of it. It's comforting to have this place ready for us. I just don't want to beat her to the grave. That would kill her. So I have to develop the life wish she has always had before it's too late.

The Next Day

People with bipolar disorder have an annual suicide rate twenty times that of the general population, so let's go there. If I could plan my death, I would want to die in the morning, sitting in meditation. I would want my spirit to have elevated into a state of bliss before deciding to remain there ... so deep in meditation that I just wouldn't return to the body. My body dies, not me.

I'm only forty-five, but I am so tired of this body. I don't want to creep out my daughters with too much death preparation, but they know I'm an earthquake freak, so what's the difference? To me it's scarier not to prepare them for the inevitable. Why shouldn't they know what I would have wanted? *Died in meditation rather than in her sleep*, the coroner's office will report. How did they know? "Her eyes were open. She died awake," they'll say. "Not in her sleep. Just as she planned."

I've already told my daughters that I would be visiting them after I'm gone. "It will be at 4:00 a.m.," I said. They rolled their eyes. It's my favorite time of day, but they don't want to be awakened. "Too bad," I said. "I'll be waking you up. At 4:00 a.m."

This is the new date; it marks my renewed abstinence from overeating. For six months, I've been trying to blot out my existence, or at least dull it, with food. Food addiction makes a person want to die. Some say you want to die first, and then you overeat. It's the chicken-or-egg dilemma, when really both are true. Wanting to die isn't about life situations, the people in my life, or ingratitude. It isn't about not having anything or not having enough to live for. It isn't about "How could she do that to her children?" Wanting to die is about seeking a spiritual connection I'm not finding here; therefore, it must be available in death.

How do we lose our way so that we don't experience heaven on earth? I have lost my way, so I know exactly what that feels like. The loss, through disconnection or disassociation, is so powerful in its disillusionment that I come to believe heaven doesn't exist and then try to search for it. Overeating is a tangible way to seek a spiritual connection. That's why it takes so much food to get there and we're never satisfied. So we die from problems directly related to overeating (maybe the heart gives out) or indirectly related. In my case, no one would suspect that a thirty-pound weight gain in six weeks means I'm living a death wish that will come out sideways through a car crash related to my fatal reply when I'm asked at the In and Out drive-through window, "Will you be eating in the car?"

I can't see my way to God. Desperate for that connection, I reach for food in an attempt to find God. In many ways, food addiction resembles a spiritual experience in its few seconds of bliss, which are better than no seconds at all. Spiritual crumbs, in communion with the ultimate "ahh," like a sensuous chocolate commercial. I feel so desperate for the perceived lost union that I reach for the connection in ways that feel prenatal but provide a sense of control over my environment. Unfortunately, discovering the reasons behind overeating has never kept me from it and neither do the enormous, debilitating, and demoralizing consequences.

What does keep me from it? I've learned that my own actions keep me from overeating. If I rely on a higher power to prevent it, and my higher power is food, I will use that food to keep me from overeating. This perpetuates the cycle until it meets a dead end. But if I'm willing to let go of the thread of spiritual connection and live in limbo for a while as withdrawal removes me from the land of disillusionment, something else takes its place. It becomes a wish to live, which always feels better than a death wish.

I've read that my relationship with God is my relationship with food. In that case, here's mine. Food has been there my entire life. Before and after, as well. I rely on it without question, knowing it will work for me even when it produces great suffering. I prefer food (and God) over people and would rather go to food (and God) than to any person. And I would perish without it. My life depends upon it. We can certainly stay alive without alcohol or tobacco, but we can't live without food (our God), and so we eat. But in the choices of the foods I eat and the amounts, herein lies my salvation. I need to drink water but don't have to choose to drink alcohol. I have to eat food but can choose the kinds and amounts. Then there's the choice of "more" than what is needed, a kind of God gluttony, as if there isn't enough of anything to go around, and I gotta get mine.

Two Weeks Later

Graveside, Gateway Memorial Park

When it comes to people, I feel no greater love than the love I feel for my daughters. It's a love so intense it pierces my heart and causes it to ache. It's unconditional and undying. I hope they feel this love from me. For some reason, I didn't (and don't) feel my parents' love, even though I know they love me. It isn't their fault that I don't feel it.

I believe it has to do with my alcoholism, once defined to me as an inability to feel and experience love. It is still that way after twenty-two years of sobriety, because food addiction numbs the heart. Because it's numb, you aren't aware of the numbness. Addictive illness is a family disease, so this concerns me. What if my daughters don't feel this great love I have for them? They know I love them, and I say it daily, but do they *feel* that I love them? I feel my daughters' love for me, that's for sure. I feel my love for my parents. Whether my parents feel my love for them, I would be too afraid to ask. What if their answer is no? We'd all be devastated by such revelations. Or maybe the love would pour into us while tears pour out of us.

I'm here today, noticing that my other neighbor got fresh plastic tulips and a Father's Day balloon. These neighbors are a couple. *Oh, my.* She is still alive! He died in April of 2009. She just had her eightieth birthday. He was in the Marine Corps, and the flag for July 4 is already up. Or maybe it was placed there for Memorial Day. Or both. Carved on their marker are the words "They whom we love and lose are no longer where they were before. They are now wherever we are." That's a reference to hidden dimensions in string theory in the realm of quantum physics, and I'll bet this couple didn't even know it. But it isn't complete without this addendum: Alive, they are also wherever we are; we just don't notice it, because we only comprehend spatial concepts, such as Redlands is a two-hour drive from La Jolla.

I could contact the wife. She and I are both alive and will be neighbors forever one day. She could even meet my mom, also eighty. Would they think this odd? I'd better make up my mind fast; she could join her hubby at any time. One day my children and this couple's descendants could arrive at the same time and meet while visiting us.

Back to string theory. "I am already dead also" is a perspective from the theory of everything's no-time, no-space philosophy. I believe dead is also alive anyway. Dead just means I left my body. But I don't have to die for my spirit to go or be everywhere. Death is not a requirement for this. My spirit is already everywhere, and it moves within this body, as well. It's just not limited to it.

It takes practice to wrap a brain around this notion, but it's so enlightening and true. After death, we try to sense a person's presence, and we find it. Alive, we aren't searching for them in this way. We don't sense people. We know they're at work or at home, out of town or a phone call away. We can search for the actual presence of anybody while they're alive. So why would we seek to sense them with us? What would be the purpose unless they're dead? Well, what is the purpose *after* they're dead? We want to *know* they are with us. Why can't we operate under the same purpose when they're alive? Kind of puts a new spin on loneliness if all you have to do is call up the sense of somebody.

I love my resting place. Here, my words get eternalized. Elsewhere, they just end up on a page.

Forty Days Later

AUGUST 5, 2011
Graveside, Gateway Memorial Park

Here it is Friday night, and I'm trying to beat traffic to get to the cemetery before dusk, when it closes. Don't these drivers know I have a date with death? On a Friday evening, my resting place is the quietest spot in our culture. And there's no cover charge. Hard to find parking, though. Do they not want people loitering? I shimmy up next to someone's marker, which is too close to the asphalt. *What were they thinking?* I worry that I could run them over and squash them, but then I remember they are already dead. Can't die in any more car accidents.

How sweet! Someone planted impatiens near my plot, and there appears to be a new tree that could potentially uproot my stone in fifty years. Is someone already visiting me before I'm here?

Yes. The gardener. But why that location for the tree sprig? It seems deliberate rather than part of a general landscaping plan. Who was it?

I wonder if the quotation on my neighbors' headstone needs to be edited. Instead of "They whom we love and lose are no

longer where they were before. They are now wherever we are,"
it should say, "They whom we love are wherever we are." Dead
or alive, so lose the word *lose*.

People! It's the first time I've seen anyone but me visit my
neighborhood. "Hi, Grandpa!" the little boy says, touching the
nameplate on the stone wall. Oh, no, they're whispering now.
Darn it, I can't hear what else they're saying. I wanted to over-
hear their conversation. Who, why here, why now?

They must have seen the invisible sign all cemeteries post:
Quiet, please. There's some stupid, unwritten rule about being
respectful and quiet in such settings so as not to disturb. It's
not like we're going to wake anyone up. It should be like any
other social arena where it is socially acceptable to mingle and
make small talk, asking questions like "What did your relative
die from?"

You're not allowed to be happy in a place like this. Your face is
supposed to be somber and contemplative, and your gait should
be slow. No deadlines allowed. Dancing in a cemetery doesn't
make sense unless you're drunk on Halloween and trying to re-
enact Michael Jackson's *Thriller*.

I want to tell these people, "Hey, come see my plot over here!"
But can you imagine? They'd call a 5150 on me. How transparent it would be to them that I have skipped the actual suicidal
act and came here to crawl right under my stone and bury myself
alive.

Another visitor, a man! Oooooh, dark glasses. Don't ever let
'em see you cry. Do I dare? What do I dare if I do dare? He's
dusting a marker on the same stone wall, but it's a different
plaque. After he leaves, I'll read it.

He walks away, checking phone messages. Yep, from here I

can see her name on the marker. He looks to be in his twenties. Drug overdose? Breast cancer? Car accident? "How did she die?" That's what I want to ask.

I think that's called morbid curiosity. No, my dare isn't what I want to ask but what I want to tell him: "You know, she's still with you."

That comment alone could dig two disastrous pitfalls, either of which could put me six feet under: (1) "Excuse me? None of your (expletive) business." or (2)"What did you say?" in a shaming tone. Wait, three pitfalls. No response would be the gravest one of all. But it might be a dare worth the risk for the flip side. What if the man broke down weeping because in his heart he knows it's true and now someone else has confirmed it for him in her presence? And what if he leaves the cemetery with her spirit more alive in his heart?

Too late anyway. He's already driven off in his blue truck with a washing machine loaded in back. A washer she will never use. Okay, so it's time to sneak a peek at her marker. Holy Moses! Why did I think it was his girlfriend? Judging by the dates and his age, she must be his mom. "Always in our hearts," it says. So he already knows she's with him. I wouldn't have given him any new information. Not so daring of me after all.

Let me think of a bigger dare. Okay, here it is. "How do you experience her being with you still?" That's it! My assignment is to work up the courage to chitchat with one of my neighbor's living relatives and risk asking that question. The thing is, how is that answer any different in death than in life? Wouldn't they be with us in those same ways while alive? Maybe the ways in which they've always been with us, in addition to the ways we experienced them with us, just become more evident after death.

I'll come up with some examples and return to this. But my point is that maybe if we noticed those ways while people are alive, we would have a completely different grief experience. Maybe we would view loss in another way, if we felt a sense of loss at all.

For now, it's nearing dusk. One day I want to find out how long I can stay here before someone kicks me out. I'll pretend not to know they aren't open 24/7 like drive-throughs. According to the park office, dusk is when the sun goes down. But they couldn't tell me how long it is until the gateway to heaven closes.

The sun is peeking through the pines. Pine trees are perfect for cemeteries, because we can pine in the sense of wailing or crying or longing. But do it quietly, of course. Oh, wow, the low sun shines directly upon my marker! The sun sets on my stone out of all the others! How heavenly.

I wonder if anyone else does the same thing I do: Visit his or her own site like people visit the sites of others. Okay, so there's no parking, no seating, and you can't very well sit on the memorial benches people buy in place of markers. I'm glad I got the plot next to the steps. I did that on purpose so that people who visit can have a place to sit next to me.

The Next Day

Graveside, Gateway Memorial Park

I get here and see that someone's coffee cup is sitting on their marker. That's a diehard Starbucks addict. A couple is planting their own plant beside a marker. "Can we do that?" I ask. They reply, "No one's said anything."

That's how it should be in life, too. Go for it and only stop if someone says something to you, and even then ...

That gives me a great idea. I don't like impatiens. But they'll die on their own anyway, because they aren't hardy plants. So I will secretly bring morning glory seeds to sprinkle around my marker. Hee hee! You understand, right? These flowers are considered weeds, because they grow so heartily and under any and all conditions. Even when you try to kill them all, there's a speck that survives somewhere in the dirt, and they grow back even heartier than before. So one day the morning glories from my plot will take over the neighborhood. Well, they won't get far. Memorial parks are notorious for meticulous landscaping. But that won't stop me. Morning glories are wild and unwieldy, which is why I love them. They don't care what anyone else thinks. They are undaunted; they are who they are, and they can't be killed off. Next visit, seeds.

The self-imposed rule about me writing only at my marker is very inconvenient. It's not like a brief rest at a cemetery suits my multitasking personality. If I could figure out how to move my resting place from here into all other areas of my life, I could carry this journal with me wherever I go. But that feels like cheating, like faking it. I do jot down ideas for what I want to write about when I come here, but I end up writing something else anyway. So far, I haven't even borrowed from those notes. All I know is that today I didn't really want to come, feeling tired and too busy. But after being here a short time, I'm well rested. Let's see, that took fifteen minutes.

The Next Day

Oh, my God. This place is dead on a Sunday. I thought for sure I'd have to fight traffic. It must be only that way on Mother's Day, Father's Day, Memorial Day, and Veteran's Day.

Guess what? This is my new church. When people ask where I go to church, I'm going to say it's a place nearby called The Resting Place. I'll leave out that it's in Gateway Memorial Park. I'll see if the conversation goes beyond that.

People ask, "Do you go to church?" either because they don't want to be alone in their churchgoing, knowing everything else they could be doing, or they are trying to save you. I got tired of explaining my church history, and I've never asked anyone if they go to church. However, I can tell that no one has been envious of the reasons I don't go. I love being at home on a Sunday with my girls, and when I'm alone, I love being at home on a Sunday with myself. Besides, now that I've found my resting place, I can come here during regular and extended business hours, longer than any church doors are open. My point being, I have found my sacred place of worship. I'm not quite sure yet what

I'm worshipping. It looks like I'm worshipping death, but I think I am worshipping life, aka God, if God is indeed life and indeed love. If so, my resting place is where I come to worship life and love. Good enough for now.

At home I panicked that I could die before I planted those morning glory seeds I wrote about yesterday. That's why I'm back so soon. But I'm terrified of getting caught by the surveillance camera. I wonder what the fines are for unapproved planting and if it's considered vandalism. I'll do the deed just before I leave so I can make a quick exit.

I plucked a yellow flower from my front yard at home, my first fresh flower to adorn my own plot. Has anyone else ever done this? Do you know how good it felt to do it? Once I die, I won't be able to bring flowers to my plot. In some ways, I'm doing things now that are impossible for dead people. It makes me feel I have transcended death temporarily or at least entered eternity for a brief moment. No, I've crossed the boundaries between life and death. That's it. I've returned from the dead before I've even left by placing a flower on my own plot.

The fate of the yellow flower defied intention. I was driving to my resting place when my former mother-in-law's plot called to me. *Oh, the flower is for her, not me. I see.* It's been a long time since I visited her grave site. It was my idea to put the marker there in the 1990s, but I can't go there right now. She's the mother of my children's father, and I still call her my mother-in-law. Her son and I divorced in October of 2008. She died from breast cancer when he was seven. I can't say any more yet. What I need to say now is "The yellow flower means I'm sorry for his broken heart. I feel you are proud of how we parent and that we get along well enough that our family life feels whole in spite of the split. I'm sorry your granddaughters' hearts were broken, as well. Breaking three little-girl hearts was devastating. May God fill the spaces where we are all broken." *I almost forgot myself.* "I'm sorry for my broken heart, too." I guess I went there after all.

I don't like yellow anyway. Why would I bring a yellow flower for my plot? But you know what I did do? I put a few morning glory seeds in my hand and shoved them into the dirt with my thumb next to her plot. Now I'm going to keep watch. The little packet says ten days to germinate, fifty to eighty days to bloom, and they grow twelve feet in full sun.

Oops! Six inches apart? No one told me! I inserted a dozen all together in one push. But we've got the full sun. No one here needs sunscreen, and all the plots see the light of day until after dusk. Instead of growing twelve feet tall, maybe it will crawl twelve feet! Fifty days from now is the end of September. Okay! I'll be on the lookout for sprouts come fall.

A falcon! Perched on a nearby guardrail.

Tom, you show-off. Tom's not buried here. I don't know where Tom is buried yet. But since this adoptive father to a brother I didn't grow up with died in a plane crash on January 10, he's been flying everywhere, appearing as birds to several of his loved ones. It's happened so often that we call it bird watching and share field notes by email. Only this time, I'm not feeling anything from the falcon, so let me put the pen down.

Damn! A huge insect just flew at me. I jumped, and there went Tom.

I wish the bugs here were dead, too. I did get the message in time, however. "Don't forget me in your journal," he said. Tom's is an amazing story for any resting place. He was and is evidence that we are everywhere, hence his bird morphing. His perspectives on life and death are intertwined. He is the most alive dead person I know. He was the most alive person I knew while he was alive. He loved life, and now, obviously, he's loving death. As soon as I think of him, he's here with me. By his invention, Tom, the judge, was the only lifetime member of Early Risers International, my club for early risers. I only charged twenty-five cents a year for membership, but he insisted on giving me $25. That was in 1997, when he figured on 100 years of membership. "It will carry me into the afterlife," he said. I had wanted to put him in my early rising book called *Morning Glory*, but I never wrote the book, and now he's dead.

After his death, I called upon him to help me write what he would say at his own memorial service. Out popped a poem I swear he used my hand to write. "May you feel my presence in your hour of grief, when the 3:00 a.m. hour steals sleep like a thief. May you walk in my footsteps; I'll show you the way. When the road gets too rough, know I'm here to stay. May you feel my presence in your hour of joy, when you think of me as a man or a boy. May you listen intently to the silence at hand. When you hear the One Voice, you'll understand. May you care for each other, as I have for you, when you hold in your hearts the truth that is true."

It's just nice to know that Tom may be buried somewhere in Illinois where he lived, but he still loves to travel. I met Tom after I met his adopted son, Eric, who shares the same birth father with me. Until almost age thirty, Eric was a boy out there our father knew about but never met. Eric and I flew back to the memorial services for Tom in Illinois. I got to sit in Tom's chair in the courtroom and read his poem. I felt like his adopted daughter, Eric being my brother.

After I finished paying respects to my mother-in-law's relatives' broken hearts, all five of us, I walked past the plot where the couple planted greenery yesterday. I wish I had seen their marker, because I might have dared to ask the question: "How do you experience her being with you still?" She was only three. "Our angel from heaven." The dates say sunrise 2007 to sunset 2010. What are the chances I'll run into this couple again? I'm going to leave a tiny note in their shrine to her. Is that done? "Dear parents, may I please talk to you about your daughter? I was the one you met yesterday who asked you about planting plants, and I own a nearby plot."

Will I get busted for treating the cemetery like a community bulletin board? How come there's no social networking going on here? No one says a word to anyone, and our relatives are spending eternity together. This is common ground for our families to share for generations. How tragic!

That's it. I'm redoubling my efforts. Living relatives of the neighboring deceased, here I come. I'll start with my two closest neighbors.

I had a sickening thought on the way to my plot today. What if my mom dies first? She's going to be eighty-one on October 1 and is as healthy as a horse, but she has chosen not to have mammograms for decades now. I know why, even though she won't say. If she has cancer, she doesn't want chemo, pity, or suffering. She doesn't want to be a burden to anyone. She wants it to be Stage IV if detected, with only weeks to live. I'll bet she has a plan to ensure her death should she catch wind that she might have to undergo any type of painful existence. I'm really too afraid to ask her what she has in mind.

I wouldn't want to die before my mom, because I wouldn't want her to suffer the pain of losing a daughter. But when I bought the plot, it was just mine, and I wasn't thinking of her death. Now, because she's in on it, it's just a matter of time before we know who gets to go on the page first. So the sickening thought was *What if I'm not ready in time for her death?* And what in hell does *ready* mean? All I know is it made me feel sick to my stomach.

I gotta get outta here. Now I know why this place is dead on a Sunday. I'm going home.

I've planted my *Ipomoea Tricolor* heavenly blue morning glory seeds, and I washed my marker. The flowers will be ready by my mother's birthday. By the way, she asked to see the plot next time she's in the area.

Here come two people. I'm just not up for socializing today.

The Next Day

Upon arrival, I notice someone else with a secret death wish besides me! A woman in her mid-forties, with a forlorn face, is pacing slowly as if looking for somebody. Smoking! If only she knew she was just looking for herself and that quitting smoking could be a first step. Can you imagine if I were to say that to her? Would she hit me? The unknown potential of her reaction keeps me silent.

How do we dare speak what we really feel in our hearts and minds? First, how do we even identify what we feel? And what do we do if we think we are feeling and communicating but are only fooling ourselves?

What do I want to say (or at least admit to myself) today, screening out what might be called *harmful truthful communication*, which is a lie because of its intent to injure rather than communicate? That's why they refer to it as brutal honesty. Truth frees. It hurts sometimes but conveys love. I really wish I could hug my children's father, for example. But what are my motives? If my intent is to recapture what we had and rope him back in or interfere with what he has now due to some underlying anger, I'd better do nothing and keep quiet. If my motive is to avoid grief by hugging him, because deep down I feel the loss of the relationship and call it "missing him," I temporarily sidestep a clean grieving process. Okay, no hug. Not today.

I do want to get him a birthday present. Starbucks card? No. Coffee connects me to him the most, which is why since January it's been my favorite binge beverage ... rich, dark, smooth, and sweet. Banana walnut bread to go with it. It's the exact combo I enjoyed more than twenty years ago with my children's father on the East Coast, before we were married and before I got help for my eating problems.

We took turns. He would visit me in Washington, D.C., where I worked for USA Today, and I would visit him in New York, where he worked for Newsday. It was so romantic that during the week I would down pints of Häagen Dazs Vanilla Swiss Almond to the point of suicidal feelings. He wanted to marry me anyway, and when I told him, "Not for at least five years," I knew it was because the ice cream had me. That's because love was all too scary.

Back to coffee. I loved how it tasted when we kissed in the morning after breakfast, all through our twenty years together. Somewhere along the line, coffee became breakfast. At least, that was true for him. I had to give it up after abusing coffee to the point of breast lumps resembling the driving range at a golf course. My doctor said they'd reduce and perhaps even disappear if I gave up caffeine. So I switched to decaf but drank so much of it, thinking the two-percent caffeine content would add up to a buzz eventually, that coffee became acid in my stomach. Despite my coffee restriction, I learned to fix my husband's daily brew, and he was always impressed with how consistently good it was when I never tasted it.

So, in January, when I simply *had* to drink coffee for the first time in twelve years, I thought I could find him in there somewhere. But no matter how much coffee I drank, he was never at the bottom of the cup. That's why it's important for me not to give him a Starbucks gift card; it will thwart my grieving process.

Divorce is death. Three years after ours became final, I geared up for my first divorce recovery group. I showed up on schedule, but no one else was there. I had the correct day and time. At least they were the ones I was given. I felt devastated and angry; where was my support when I was finally ready for it? I decided not to go back. I'd find another place to grieve, like here.

This is the first day of my new job as the author of *The Resting Place*. The idea of my journal becoming a book grew until I accepted it as truth. I'm having so much fun writing it. This is what it must be like to be a successful writer. So let's take stock. My new office is outdoors by a rushing water fountain, my co-workers are all dead, and I get to work alone. My cubicle doesn't have walls, and the chair is made of stone. My office supplies are limited to two pens, this journal, and my cell phone. Hearing the birds sing is like listening to a nature CD or watching Tom having fun. I brought a candle to my plot today, one with a fresh pine-wreath scent. Unfortunately, I forgot to bring matches to light it.

The journey to the cemetery this morning was an adventure. I had a spontaneous urge to take the car in to be serviced. I thought it was only two miles away from here, but it was four. The serviceman kept asking (four times), "Are you sure you don't need a ride?" He couldn't believe I wanted to walk to work. I did ask for a pickup. The truth is that I felt both compelled to be here today and repelled about being here. I had to be here because … I'm not sure yet. As I started walking, I realized I had the inklings of a life wish stirring in me. I needed time to process the newness of it. The life wish happened when the sidewalk disappeared and I had to walk facing traffic in the bike lane. I feared getting hit by a car. I've fantasized before about stepping out in front of a moving vehicle, but this time I feared I wouldn't make it to the cemetery. I feared this could be the day. Well, I guess I would have made it to the cemetery either way.

A mosquito just bit me. I must bring insect repellent tomorrow.

The walk was worth the effort, because the life force promptly drew not one but two cat calls from drivers, and I don't recall that happening in the last twenty years. I guess I did dress too sexy for work. I don't know what possessed me this morning, but I picked out a close-fitting animal-print top. Don't these men know I'm still twenty pounds above my best weight? I like being just heavy enough that no one looks at me. This invisible feeling is safe because (1) I won't feel sensuality, (2) no one else will either, so (3) there will be no lovemaking. This body won't have any more sex once I'm laid in the plot. What's the difference between now and then if my big body is in a self-created coffin I've crawled into like an early grave? Either way, no sex.

For some reason, I had a really unusual fantasy last night about the cemetery. The best fantasies are the kind you don't make up but that come out of the blue. They're so real it's like being in another dimension or a parallel universe and so detailed it feels like it's actually happening.

Oh, my God, where do I go to the bathroom? I wish I could pee in the bushes, but the surveillance camera …

Anyway, the fantasy. Andrew Fletcher walks up to my garden district, and I'm sitting here in my office. He is drop-dead gorgeous. Dark hair, tall, with an athletic build, and I can't even see his eyes yet. *A white doctor's coat? Don't they usually take those off before they get to the medical center parking lot?* He slows his pace as he walks toward me. I can't help but smile; that relaxes his approach some. Surely he felt that secret code of respect and didn't want to intrude on … what, my death wish? We don't even say hello for some reason. But his smile lights up his eyes *(I can see now that they are green)*, and I travel into the windows of his soul. Of course, this heavenly glimpse causes me to avert my gaze and pretend I'm writing. I write, "Oh, my God, what do I say? I have to say something to this man, but my breath has been taken away." It's not like my written words will leap off the page. *He swipes his hand across the dates on my neighbor's marker. He has to be her son! My neighbor's son!* Truth or dare. No, dare the truth. What do I say? God help me now, or forever hold my peace; come on, word woman, give it to me now. "Hi" seems so empty at a time like this.

Then it comes out of its own accord. "You're her son."

"You knew her?"

"I wanted to find her, because she's going to be my mother's neighbor."

I don't dare tell him it's my plot, too. But I do risk adding, "My mom isn't dead yet. Is there time for them to meet?"

The way he looks at me …

Commercial break. Gardener approaches. "Por favor, el baño acerca de aquí?" He gestures "that way." Of course, I get lost on foot; I have no sense of direction. He yells "El baño!" and points opposite the way I'm going. But the sign says Authorized Personnel Only. I guess I'm an employee after all. I get to go where the gardeners go. I see trucks with shovels in dirt. Oh, my God, what if they're gravediggers, too. Whatever they're called, they are so good at watering the grounds it's no wonder many cemeteries are called Evergreen, like my grandfather's site in Tucson, Arizona. That reminds me (now that I see how wet it is) that I have to put my note to the three-year-old's parents in a plastic baggie. Glad I didn't leave it yesterday.

Dr. Andrew Fletcher faded like a ghost as soon as nature called.

I found a yellow silk rosebud with no stem about ten feet from my plot. Since it wasn't around any other plot, it's finders keepers, and picking up waste is a community service. A yellow rose? I hate yellow. Oh, but Mom likes yellow, so it's for her. Wait. Which half of the plot do I put it on? Is she going to be on the right or the left? I get to decide one of two ways. Either she dies first, or I make a note in the office file that I want to be buried on the right side of the page.

There are too many bees here. What was I thinking?

I can't get stung to death after I become a full-time resident, but the fear of it now will kill me before anaphylactic shock. I'll have to bring an EpiPen™ to the office tomorrow. How ironic that my name in Greek means "all honey." Bees are attracted to me; I am deathly afraid of myself.

Hawk! Does Tom hang out here as much as I do? Or does he just do a flyby when I'm here? This flyby sent me a message: I'm still here!

The reason I want the right side of the page is that I am right-handed and do not like writing on the left side of journal pages. My mom, I'll tell you, could care less, because she's an artist not a writer, and her page will be blank like a canvas or with a picture and no writing at all. What picture? Painting? Artwork? I can't ask her. But I could ask the office what options are available. If our plot comes up again in conversation with my mother, I'll tell her about those options unassumingly. I'll let her know that I'm putting "She rose in the forelight" on mine.

Mom wrote in high school ... oh, my God, that's it! I'm reading that one at her eulogy. I need to find out how many words I can get on her gravestone page. Here are her words:

No Wind, No Rock, No Reef

When stars like tears of sorrow are falling everywhere,
And their streams of light and splendor fill the cool,
 crisp blue-black air,
I long to sail the heavens, ride o'er those waves of grief.
No obstacle may stop me, no wind, no rock, no reef.
The Milky Way my course will be, the North Star is my guide,
And I, alone, I sail the sky -- Diana at my side.

    —Mary Moore, Sunset Hill School,
     Kansas City, MO, 1947

Okay, so the yellow silk rose is in front of Mom's left side. My mother. I can't wait to be here with her forever. We'll get along so well and never have a fight. Inches apart, closer than we've ever come for longer than we've ever been, friends forever! For nine months, I grew inside my mother. So she is the closest I'll ever get to any human. Technically, no matter how far apart I think we are, even if we're on opposite pages, I was closer to her physically than I ever was to another human being. Even my daughters were limited to being only in my womb. My entire body was inside my mother's.

A bee is eating a slug one foot from my leg. I froze instead of freaking, and it went away. I faced my deathly fear and lived!

I feel closer to my daughters than any other people in the world. With these three girls, I experience physical, emotional, mental, and spiritual closeness. We have the relationship every mother should have with a daughter. I am so blessed. Why would I ever leave my girls without their mother? In my darkest moments, I've asked myself this question out of horrified guilt. I don't know the answer yet. Enough on that topic.

Oh, my God, I didn't know this book would be so heavy. How am I going to keep up this kind of consciousness? Life and love are so overwhelming in their mystery, joy, pain, wonder, and power, and I just want to climb into my plot now. Bury myself alive. It's why I've overeaten in the past. I actually prefer living closer to death than to life. I don't fully understand why, when life is so good. I understand when life sucks why you wouldn't want to live. They tell me it's chemicals, and I can't help it. But that's too easy an answer. And that answer alone doesn't produce the necessary life wish.

I'm outta here. The bees are getting aggressive.

I forgot to mention that on the walk up, I noticed the names of a couple engraved on a marker. They were in their forties when they died on the same day. They were for sure a couple, because their heart symbols are linked. Car accident? It must have been. What else could it be? Car accidents top double murders. It could've been me dying on the road today, a step away from my grave, either intentionally or due to an accident because I took such a huge risk walking here this morning, daring to do something I've never done before. The trouble with risk is it could lead to death. But even if I don't take risks, I'm still going to die. Ergo, all actions lead to death.

What risks will I take today (or not take) to live fully in the rest of my day? I won't risk my life by taking that first compulsive bite or drink, even though drinking isn't pressing at the moment like food has been. I won't take risks on the road. I won't run the risk of injuring my children by pushing them too fast in life, interrupting them, using "the rough voice" I'm accused of using several times a week. And I won't run the risk of alienating my youngest by not playing with her today.

I will risk asking for what I need. Asking for help. Giving love. Telling the truth. Breathing deeply. That's enough risk for today.

Sorry I cut short the fantasy about Dr. Andrew Fletcher. But that's the nature of fantasy. "Poof!" So there. Maybe he'll return at another time.

I'm going to go hang out with my children's grandmother until my ride from the auto center comes. She's closer to the entrance, and I've rested here enough for today.

Here's a quote from another couple's marker near mine. He died three months ago. She didn't. Late seventies. One marker says, "I'll see you in the morning." The other displays the words "To live in the hearts of others is not to die." We're all visiting cemeteries when we could just look into our own hearts for these people, feeling and seeing everyone. If I have the opportunity to return here tomorrow, I hope I have enough courage.

Two Days Later

AUGUST 10, 2011
Graveside, Gateway Memorial Park

I came to work today feeling disorganized in mind, body, and spirit, and when I got here, my mom's rose was gone and so was my evergreen candle. Thieves! I must be breaking the rules. Oh, now I see them, scattered nearby. It looks like someone just kicked them a few feet away. Anyway, I'm glad I was only gone for a day.

I forgot the matches again. Wait, maybe I have some in the car. I need a sweater anyway. But what if they see me light the candle and it's against the rules and I look like an arsonist or I forget to blow it out and the garden district burns down? That happened to my home when I was growing up. If I burn down my neighborhood here, I could be put in jail, and I wouldn't get to pick up my girls.

So forget the match. A sweater's harmless. Be right back.

I'm full of random thoughts and feelings this morning. I don't know how much of it matters, so I don't know where to begin. Perhaps I should begin with the panic attacks. So what if my children's father was supposed to be on the other page of my plot so the girls could always visit us together, even though we're not married anymore? I wanted to grow old with him, even after we divorced. I can't ask him, because that would open me up to further (now eternal) rejection. He might say, "I don't even want to be with you in death." And if he said yes, my mom would feel preempted and displaced. But I wouldn't tell her, which means I'd feel guilty for all time, like I betrayed her trust and her investment.

I do know that he plans to end up in this park, because it says so in his will and because his mother is here. He knows I'll be here, but he doesn't know I already bought a plot. I came into this world with my mom, and I want to leave here with her. But I haven't seen any other mother-daughter plots. It's only couples. So are parent-child combos not politically correct? Is it incestuous or socially backward or against the norm? Will I regret it once I meet the good doctor and his mother-in-law is in the way for all eternity? It's maddening that, ultimately, I cannot manage what gets done in the end. I have no control over life's terms, and I've no control over death. I can only plan.

Do we intuitively know when we are about to die? I'm here daily, working as if I have a deadline. I don't control that either. Oh, I know what I can do. If Mom's here first, and I change my mind later, her poodle Puffy, who looks like Einstein, can go here. They allow pets to be buried in their own spots. They just can't be cremated with you and placed in your urn. But Mom might never know whether it was Puffy who ended up next to her or me. I think she would prefer Puffy. He's definitely gotten closer to my mother in her golden years than anyone else.

Wait. This is my resting place. That's the whole point! Why am I so willing to give up my place in the world even in death? Because I displace myself all the time in life, separating from what I really believe, think, and feel, as if I do not have a right to be here. Typical.

I need some authenticity right now. At least before I die, so I can say I was almost true to myself. So let me try to capture a few of my random thoughts. My first daughter already knew at a young age that "be true to yourself" was a valid lifelong goal. In her sixth-grade graduation statement, she wrote that her goal in life was to be herself. Everyone else chose occupations and world-saving ambitions. How did she know that her statement is perhaps the highest aspiration any of us can ever aim for in life? As well as the most challenging? Probably because she's so good at being herself.

Back to the random. I brought the baggie for the note to the three-year-old's parents. I dressed in sweats today, so I hope I don't run into the good doctor at work this morning. The future guy came to me one night in a dream. It was the best lovemaking of my life. Who is this guy who came alive at the cemetery and now visits me in my bedroom? Andrew Fletcher. A name out of the blue. This is no different from when I was twelve years old and wrote the name of my imaginary future husband in my address book, along with a fake phone number. Then I ended up marrying a man with the right first name but wrong last name. No, that didn't mean he was the wrong man. People always seem to justify their divorces by claiming they married the wrong man or woman. Why? Just because you divorce doesn't make the entire marriage a mistake, unless it was one. My marriage was deliberate, intentional, and mindful. For the record, so were the calculated conceptions of each child.

So much happened yesterday when I did not come here. I met with John, a career counselor, and we prioritized my life. Motherhood is my only priority. Then comes work. I want to publish a series of books about divorce called *Soul Custody,* the first titled *Daily Meditations for Single Mothers.* Then comes professional development. I'm trying to learn Facebook and social media marketing and establish a website for book sales. It feels like *The Resting Place* will shape everything that follows, paving the way for everything else and putting it all into focus so I can live from who and what I really am. Plus, it's the only avenue right now where the words are flowing. At the moment, I can only do it when I sit here. That's why I've made this my office.

I forgot the mosquito repellent. It's a cold and dreary summer day. I have two hours to rest.

In meditation at home this morning, I had rolled from my sitting position onto the floor. Tom came and lifted me off the floor, where I lay like a dead body. He said I had to get to work. I feel dead at home and alive at my resting place. I have it all backward. He said it had to change. This stark realization is like coming to a truth you feared all along. I've not wanted to be here for as long as I can recall. I can't wait until I die so I can shed this prison of mine. My spirit feels defiled, crushed, broken, and unfixable because of my human experiences, and I want out. Except for my three daughters. I live for them, and I want to live for them as long as possible. So I eat right (by default, not due to perfection or virtue), exercise, and take care of myself. I want to be here because I am their mother, the best mother for them, and God gave them to me to raise. I love them, and they love me, so *The Resting Place* just supports motherhood.

I didn't tell John that this book comes before my professional development and the job search I'm supposed to be cultivating. I wanted to give him the more pragmatic answer. That's because if I don't confront this death wish, the rest of my life won't be very much alive. Only after *The Resting Place* is written will I be able to make better choices. I was appalled when meeting with John to discover that I already have everything I could possibly need or want in life, including the resources, background, and experience to follow through on my heart's desires. Everything is at my disposal. I am appalled by the way I spend the majority of my time ignoring, avoiding, running from, and escaping people, places, and opportunities, even though I see myself as a go-getter. I'm really a go-forgetter. It's chronic, a disease that is debilitating, crippling, and self-sabotaging.

Up until now. *The Resting Place* has given me new life and perspectives that have started to change me in ways I've not previously known. My intention is to put my life into focus here. I'll write about motherhood and daughters and work. I'll reflect upon and project the new focus onto my life. My intention is to walk away a live woman by the end of this book. I came here with breath and a heartbeat I didn't realize I had. I was already dead but didn't even know it. Each time I write here, I leave a little bit—no, a lot more—alive, and I can't wait to come back for more.

I have no intention of dying. When I leave this life (or should I say when I climb into my plot), I have plans and designs of universal proportions. The first being to keep watch over all my girls throughout their lives and the lives of their children. How long do we live? Can I be present with the entire lineage? Just keep going endlessly? Can I go backward into my past lineage? Can I really go anywhere, anytime, like Tom says? My littlest girl says that after I die, she'll hug me in her heart. She's four and has it all figured out.

Maybe what we really miss or cry about after a loved one dies is that we can't touch each other ever again in the physical sense. But we hardly touch each other in our living days, so how can that be the reason? Maybe it's that we regret not touching them enough physically when they were alive, when we could have done so. Maybe we weren't touched enough by them or in the right ways. We do say people touched our hearts, which they actually can't do physically unless they're heart surgeons. Since we don't get it that the people are still with us, we say those who think that way are in denial. "She hasn't accepted yet that he's gone. She talks about him in present tense as if he's still alive." Well, she's probably right. We should be crying hard now for the folks who don't know she's right.

This is suddenly all too heavy for me. What happened to my random thoughts? They washed away in the garden waterfall. I have a sudden desire to run through the sprinklers, but I wouldn't want to get my clothes wet, which means I'd have to take them off to do it, which means the surveillance camera would record the scene ...

It's my lotion that's attracting the bees! Okay, no more wearing the scent of oatmeal and shea butter to work.

If I were to run through the sprinklers naked, it might attract the good doctor, if he showed up. It also might get me locked up, and I wouldn't be able to pick up my girls today at 10:30. Better just sit still.

Running through the sprinklers on the quad at the University of Redlands is socially acceptable if you're wearing a bathing suit. I've been meaning to find out the watering times so I can time my visit. I'll call today if I don't forget!

What else has been causing me panic attacks since work

began? As I was saying, I was sad I might not get to meet my neighbors here, and then I felt the same way about the neighbors in my housing complex at home. So I've devised a socially acceptable plan to meet all of them, now that I've waved politely for a year while passing by in a car.

I own an earthquake survival company called Fault Line, and I'm still improving my own family disaster plan. So I need to learn about the doctors in the neighborhood, meet the emergency-trained neighbors, and network in advance to increase our survival chances. My backyard, for example, is one of the most ideal locations to hop the fence when the power goes out on the front gate. The neighbors already know I'm on this mission; it was announced in the HOA newsletter. I just haven't done it yet, because I ran into a roadblock four months ago regarding the basic principle "love thy neighbor."

It began with a simple walk through the neighborhood. I had a vision. *What if the guy I'm supposed to meet is behind one of these doors, in one of these houses right now, and I don't even know it?* Little did I realize I had already encountered the man. So three days later I run into this guy. I had heard him speak somewhere on the topic of spirituality. Talk about touching my heart from across the room! I felt like he scooped my heart out in his hand and said, "Come to me." I was too afraid to go up front after. It was love at first sound. When my heart is touched, my head shouts the order: *Retreat!* I even left early. I ran into him again in public, and that time my heart didn't listen to me. From my mouth, out popped, "Put me in your cell phone, and next time you have a speaking engagement, can you call me?" How's that for a woman asking a man for his number?

I forget the sequence of events that followed, probably because it creates heartache. Maybe it's just the go-forgetter in me.

Anyway, I came up with some reason to call him myself. I found out he was a painter, and since I needed one for my house, it was the perfect excuse to invite him over for an estimate. When I gave him my address, he gave me his, and I learned that we lived on the same street. After he arrived, we discovered that I could see the back of his house from the top of my street. So began a one-way love affair, heartbreaking from the start. I became a texter for the first time in my life, asking him to various events and activities, to which he always replied with some version of no. You get the idea. One time, he texted me that he was with his "GF in AZ." Grandparents are the only people I've ever known to be in Arizona, including the grandfather buried in Evergreen, and my daughters' grandfather lives there now. So I texted back, "Grandfather?" He did not reply.

I kept on, falling madly in love with my own desire for him, undaunted by the lack of response. Then one day I asked the dear friend who walked me down the aisle at my wedding. "How do you know if a guy likes you?" "Just ask him," the wise man replied. So I texted the direct question, something like "Are you interested in going out with me?" Well, it turns out he thought he'd told me he had a girlfriend. He thought I was joking when I asked the grandfather (GF) question. I was devastated. I actually felt more for this guy than I had for my first love, and I didn't think that was humanly possible. I had been elevated to the position of stalker. In the end, I was proud of myself. I had never been that bold with anyone. Apparently, it's normal for a guy to pursue a woman, but a woman in pursuit is called a stalker, especially if the guy has a GF. Even if the stalker doesn't get it.

Since then, I have avoided that neighbor at all costs and haven't wanted to meet any new neighbors. Nor have I worked on my family survival plan. But since the big one is coming, I really can't let my broken heart stand in the way of earthquake preparedness for my children's survival. I must carry on.

People think broken hearts heal. I do not believe they do. God just fills the space. I think hearts have unlimited capacity for being broken. Healing is simply picking up the pieces and moving on. I had never pursued someone I wanted with such zest. It was awful and awesome. I'll never do it again. Andrew Fletcher will have to come after me. The moral of the story is love thy neighbor, but only if you learn modern technology and language first. Otherwise your heart could be broken, and no Geek Squad can fix that.

Back to random thoughts. My butt aches after an hour of sitting on stone. Time to bring a pillow to the office. I'm leaving the parents' note today. My first dare. What if they call? Well, she's my neighbor, she's three, and I want to know about her. I'll ask that important question: "In what ways do you experience her still with you?" It would be so much easier if they are outraged or offended and turn me into the office for busting some rule I don't know about. I'd be off the hook and avoid the awkwardness of having to connect with them.

I need to read the cemetery rules. I'm tiptoeing around here not knowing the ground rules, and you can't do that at work. My note to the little girl's parents will probably blow away. If a glass candle can blow away, a note in a plastic baggie will likely land on someone else's plot, or a gardener will turn it in, and I'll get in trouble for cavorting with the neighbors. I know they don't give out any information on anyone. It's all confidential. But surely there are no rules against networking.

There's no time in my day to find my neighbors here, just like there's no time to meet the living neighbors for my earthquake plan. Why? We're all so busy living. Really, we're all so busy dying in countless ways. Living from my resting place, I am more able to live. And now I don't intend to die. I am living forever. So there. There's no rush for anything.

On the contrary, there's no time to waste when it comes to the situation that demands the most attention. My eating disorder has to be arrested. No sense in landing in an early grave. Giving my attention to my girls comes after my own personal survival. How can I care for them physically in this life if I am not here? Visiting within our hearts is good for eternity, but connecting at the same time in this life is better.

I'm too cold. I have to go sit in the car.

It's almost time to pick up the girls. The other day I wrote about all the risks I would take and not take, and then I rescued my daughter, who climbed too high on a concrete wall at the pool area. I also told a stupid lie, and I breathed shallowly all day long. I couldn't get enough air. Of course, after we're planted in this garden district, we no longer have to worry about air.

I have so much to write about that this book may never end. I have a plan for outlining it that includes what to add, what to include, papers to look through, and a journal called Putting Things in Order. I want to plan my memorial service and get far enough to make a DVD to leave messages for my family. So I'd better not die today. I have to live to see this book published. In career counseling with John, I learned that what I want most through work is to help people see things from different perspectives. That's how we really shape our lives, and that's something we do have control over. I get to choose how I see everything, and no one can interfere.

I won't get here tomorrow or the next day or the next. Probably not until Monday before dusk. No, I have the girls that day. Wow. I won't make it back until next Wednesday morning, a week from now! I wonder if I can take my resting place with me somehow. Would the words still flow? This is my final resting place, but does it have to be my only? What if I were to create resting places in other areas of my life? Meditation doesn't do that for me. That's about emptying the mind, not writing. My desk at home is not a resting place. Shall I make it one? How do you create a resting place in the midst of it all? I'll experiment this week and see what happens. I just fear I won't be able to write this book anywhere but here. Or maybe what I fear is the discovery that there are no other resting places in my life. If so, I'll need to create them. And then what will that mean? What will have to change? How will I change?

Wait. What if The Resting Place is inside my heart and, therefore, with me all the time? I'll try that on for size and get back to you.

Three Days Later

When I got here, a woman was sitting in my spot with her soul mate (I imagine). She's the first person I've met who is a regular visitor here. "Most people think cemeteries are creepy," she said. "But I think they're the most peaceful places." My first cemetery friend. I took down her number. She's been coming here for fifteen years, and it's not that she visits a husband buried here. She doesn't even own a plot for herself. There must be a rule against interlopers.

I risked telling her about my plot, and the conversation quickly turned into a lecture. "You have three girls," she said, "and you've got to be here for them. You're their mommy. Especially girls." Am I so transparent here that the death wish is visible to her? I knew then that I wouldn't be calling her. Then she told me she had a son die at the age of six months and a day. Had she not continued to live through her despair, she said she wouldn't be the mother of a ten-year-old child today. So she was visiting her son's grave and using my seat as a resting place.

Today, nothing on my mind mattered once I crossed the border from the main road, where the cemetery takes over. It's like a line between heaven and earth. My earthly, logistical concerns give way to The Truth and What Really Matters.

I wonder if I lied to the woman when she asked me why I bought the plot. I said it was because of a near-death experience during my November 2008 emergency stomach surgery due to a twisted colon. It didn't feel accurate when I said it. The truth was that I was in a manic phase of bipolar disorder, a kind of mixed state where the death wish entered the manic realm, hence my spending such a large chunk of money for cemetery property. I'm finding I'm more at risk for death in the manic phase than in the depressed mode, where food does it for me. In the manic phase, I'm likely to think I can cross over and then come back, as if through a portal. I seem to be ready to experiment and learn which comes first, my life or my death. Let's see if time really exists, and let's see if I can blur the parallel universes of life and death, and let's put one foot in each realm.

I can't stand being so full of spirit, feeling so alive and happy, feeling so much love. It hurts more than any hardship. Actually, that is my definition of hardship. A life lived from love not fear, from dreams not nightmares, and from good living and loving day to day. Life at its best frightens me the most, and life seems to keep getting better, which is why I feel closer to death all the time.

Unless I'm in complete denial, and I'm really dead spiritually. Empty, alone, miserable, and fooling myself out of delusional pride. Either way, the actions required of me are the same. Show up, let go, move on. Can I not accept my good life? Why the deep need to reject it, to slay and punish myself when things work well and I experience joy and happiness? Maybe it is all chemicals; I'm designed to self-destruct. If this is true, I know where it comes from. I feel I don't deserve to be alive. I have never felt deserving of this life, and the guilt causes shame, and the imploding creates the suicidal urge where I pull everything down to the suffering level just to prove I don't deserve it. This can ruin a good day or, if taken to extreme, ruin a good life, which would then ruin the lives of three little girls and others who love me. Calling it bipolar disorder somehow makes it all acceptable.

This brings to mind an important discovery. I spend time worrying about some affliction, condition, or accident about to do me in, when I really ought to be addressing what I do have control over: causing my own death due to self-destructive habits or suicide. This issue needs to take priority. I have one mission in life: to live. It is my responsibility not to take my life no matter how dark, down, and selfish I get.

I fear someday my girls will read this, stunned to find that Mommy has had a secret death wish behind her exterior of happy functioning. They see me as well-adjusted, I hope, not even drinking or overeating. I can only tell them that this is the chemical reality of having bipolar disorder. Because they are my daughters, they're at a little higher risk for it themselves. Not understanding this, I fear they might think that because of the death wish, I really didn't love them. Perhaps they will feel shame that they didn't know I was treating mental illness with spiritual wellness every day. What would their friends think? Or they might feel pressure or anger that I only lived for them. "Get a life, Mom."

I want them to feel good that I lived for them, but what a burden to cast. They'd feel pressure to keep me alive, and suddenly they become caretakers who feel overly responsible for and guilty about anything that could possibly go wrong. And if anything unusual, adverse, or bad happens to Mommy, they'd carry the burden. They might believe they didn't do a good enough job of keeping me alive or feel I didn't love them enough or think they weren't good enough for me to live for. They'd carry that weight their entire lives. What a burden suicide places on children. That's why they say it's the ultimate selfish act. And look at all the parents who take their lives.

How do I cast full responsibility for my life back onto me, using the oxygen mask analogy to save myself first? *The Resting Place* will take care of this. By the end of this journal, I'm convinced the last word will put it all in the proper place for me. In fact, my goal is to find The Resting Place I've found here in my heart, mind, and soul ... or wherever it is located.

The last time I left here, I wondered if I could take The Resting Place with me. I had a vision of it tucked away as if in a pocket "in the heart of my mind." It would be cool if my mind had a heart, because at the rate of my speedy thinking, my pulse would indicate that I'm fully alive and awake, more so than the average human.

I took the first opportunity I had to come here, which was sooner than a week. My children's father wanted the girls an extra night for his early birthday, so I have two hours right now. I haven't done well since the last time I was here, but mostly it's what I didn't do that was "well." I didn't take that first suicidally compulsive bite of food, but I did pick at my skin, and that unleashed a series of shame chemicals that triggered the "Die!" reaction in my brain.

If I'm so thin-skinned that something so simple as that can undo me, what hope do I have of surviving myself? A scratch of the skin? But, yes, all it takes is one harmful, self-destructive gesture that defiles my body, and my spirit flies away, returning only when enough time has passed that my spirit feels it's safe to return. Usually, it takes two days after picking at my skin but longer after overeating. How easy it is to hurt myself with the slightest thing. I even (maybe especially) hurt myself with the thoughts I can't control—the unconscious ones—and the thoughts I can control, which I consciously spot and recognize as self-sabotage.

I don't believe in the devil. But I do believe in opposing forces, all emanating from the same energy field. Opposing forces (maybe more than two) that we choose to focus our energies on, whether we know it or not.

Well, I wasn't going to answer the call from my friend Heidi, but I did. Then I wasn't going to return the call from my friend Maureen, but I did. So, in essence, I've passed half an hour among the living, here among the dead. That is a very good sign.

In those calls from this resting place, I sensed a desperation for my life. Incredible heartache. Even my best friend is three thousand miles away. I'm so blessed to have this soul sister, Samara. She's writing a book on dating called *It's Just Coffee*. I told her I won't start dating until it's published. I'm kind of a one-best-friend person. Always have been. That needs to be okay and enough. Everyone else I keep at an uncomfortable distance, hence my heartache. I'm sure friends can be resting places. I just keep people far enough away.

I brought the Deep Woods mosquito repellent in a Bath and Body Works bag, and it repels them but seems to attract bees.

I recently lost someone I considered my best mom-friend. I could tell the relationship just shifted on its own. I had a feeling it would. I didn't remain connected, and that has a way of producing fallout, so when you do connect again, some trifle produces a greater fallout, and you can't reconnect. The truth is, I don't invest in friendships. I'm just "there." I don't follow the rule that says to have a friend, you have to be one. And I have every excuse society has to offer.

I'm at a turning point right now. I want to be very careful that I don't feel compelled to "be who I am" or "let it hang out" or trust or divulge to just anyone. There are too many openings for being hurt, and true friendship requires a calculated risk. *Is this person good for me?* The answer, too often, is no. Leave it to The Resting Place to enable me to say what's really on my mind, things I would never say aloud to anyone in my life unless they were dead.

The fact is, I am lonely. My children's father was my best friend ever. And everyone else is a poor substitute. That's because there is no substitution possible. People are all individuals. How can you compare their level of importance and involvement in life anyway? I just miss having the kind of friend I had in him. I could say anything, and I was more comfortable around him than anyone. And I mean *truly* comfortable. When I would hear his voice on the phone, I felt relieved and at ease, as in, "Oh, thank God it's you." For some reason, I thought we could still be friends and parents after the divorce, but it turns out we are only friendly parents together.

As I leave here today, I'm going to let it be okay that my expectations of people are way too high and that I have needs that people can't possibly meet. I have, of course, completely overlooked the flip side of the issue. This isn't the time to examine the kind of friend I am to others. I can't even be a friend to myself yet. But I did just admit to Heidi that I am a friend-ditcher, and I'm glad I've connected with her enough to reveal that. She didn't believe me, and we've had great conversations about self-deception. I lied about being a friend-ditcher, because I really am quite loyal. Maybe I'm not a friend-ditcher as much as consistent connection is hard for me. Delusion is just believing something that isn't true.

I brought my pillow to the office today. It's sunny but cold at my plot, and I keep forgetting a jacket or blanket. When fall comes, I'll really need them. I look forward to coming here in the chill, rain or shine, through fall and winter and into next spring and summer. Being at my resting place does breathe new life into me. After talking to Maureen, it became clear that my addiction relapse had to do with not taking care of my soul and spirit. Over time, I experienced a subtle decline, undetected, until the addictive substance raised the red flag.

While I was away from here, I took notes and tried to write at home. I wanted to open the advance planning memorial paperwork and begin the legacy journal that came with it, but everything got in the way. And, again, there was no resting place, because the heart-of-the-mind thing didn't last long in the midst of all the distracting stimuli of the modern world. I did find myself behaving differently, acting as if every day were the only day.

Last night, I began a class to write a business plan for my year-old, in-limbo company Fault Line. Instead of "I write survival plans for families," out popped "I'm a production company for a feature film about the Big One." Angel, the instructor, reacted favorably. "Wow, that's a first!" It's a film I want to make about what happens in Southern California when the Native American community responds to tribal visions of the coming quake. John, the career counselor, said writing family plans would help me make the money to support my dream for the film and that the film plan could be part of the overall business plan. But I want Fault Line's focus to be just the film. I left my job in education to write a screenplay about the fictional discovery of the Theory of Everything. Two months later, the April 4, 2010, earthquake in Baja, California, got me into earthquake preparedness instead.

What good is a dead screenwriter? Inspired, I changed the script to "Earthquake 2." From the perspective of the grave, I see that I had wanted the company to be just that, a one-film company. It's funny how being here is like fast forwarding life to potential regrets and still having time to press rewind and correct them before they become actual regrets. So I'm on a five-week, ten-hour mission to create a creative plan to present to a future someone to produce the film while I retain original rights to it. I provide the storyline, expert advisory board, consultants, industry analysis, survey of existing films, and maybe how well they did, so that I will have something ready for an opportunity I don't know about yet. And the title came to me, too, in the class. Same as my company: Fault Line. Duh. It started out as The Big One, which could easily confuse people as to the subject matter.

The same goes for every other work project. Reduce to the essence. This is how to focus. Narrow it down to what it really is. I'll go over my project list. I'll mix time and tenses for fun. *The Resting Place* is a ... what?

I'm supposed to pick up the girls in ten minutes!

Four Days Later

I couldn't wait to get to work this morning. Then I saw people jogging up the main road. I thought I was the only person taking advantage of the memorial park's gym membership privileges.

My note to the little girl's parents is gone. I thought of calling the woman I met here, but I would rather just run into her here. Calling cemetery visitors doesn't flow naturally in the outside world.

I've been doing some light reading. I even brought the book to work today. *Putting Things in Order: A Journal to Organize Your Life for the Next Generation.* How about organizing my life for this generation? Why should they have it all neat and tidy, while I was a mess? There are a lot of informational blanks to fill in.

I did some homework since last here, including gathering materials in one place. A suitcase, so symbolic of my trip to the afterlife. My perspective doesn't quite match what some folks believe. I feel the "afterlife" is this life in a parallel universe; therefore, it is in this world in a constant state, all the time. It's all one.

For practical reasons, I'd better describe my life "out there in the *real* world," or it really won't contrast to what I'm doing "in here." I'm forty-five, the mother of three daughters aged four, ten, and thirteen. I divorced three years ago. I live in Redlands, California, in a home I call The Citrus House. The girls' father works as a book editor and lives about fifteen minutes away. We share in the girls' lives equally. Right now, I'm writing this book, *The Resting Place.* The other two books I'm working on are *Soul Custody: Daily Meditations for Single Mothers* and *Forelight Standard Time: Daily Musings on the Theory of Everything,* a kind of daily learning curve to comprehend a world without time and space. In this moment, my ideal life as a writer is at hand, as I haven't even published anything yet. Meanwhile, I take professional development workshops through a local women's business center to pave the way for future employment and/or the ability to complete these projects.

It is beautiful here today, with the light streaming through the pines. There's a stillness I didn't notice before, or maybe that comes from within me now. I've developed a solid core since I began to visit my resting place. I'm able to sit in meditation upon rising in the morning, to the point that my thoughts disengage. But that was also helped by reading Judi Hollis' new book, *From Bagels to Buddha.*

I'm in a "thing" with Mom, so right now I regret being buried with her here. Let me just say that our relationship can be fine one moment and not the next. She gets really mad at me when I don't call her back, and I get really mad at her for calling and asking why I'm not calling her back. So I finally texted my brother to let her know I'll call back when she's not so angry. What I meant was I would call back when I wasn't so angry.

In truth, I don't mind sharing the plot with her. For some

reason, I just get angry when she expresses concern about my well-being. But she is my mother, and I like the idea of being close to her one day, when she's dead, and even closer when we're both dead, because then we will be in the Great Truth together.

I dreamt about the Great Truth in February of 1989, the night of the memorial service for my mother's mother in Tucson, Arizona. By the way, my mom's mom isn't buried at Evergreen with my mom's father; they divorced, and she preferred St. Phillip's Episcopal Church mausoleum. So in my dream the night my grandmother was buried, my mother and I were walking side by side in the desert, facing the mountains above Palm Springs, where I lived at the time. The sky opened up to heaven, and the light (just like the light in my office here this morning) shone over us like a shower. We were both in awe, like "Oh!" It was grandmother's presence, and all was well with everyone and everything, and a zillion white teddy bears emerged from the clouds.

The dream occurred after an episode where my reaction to my mother's angry grief caused me to want to bash my head against the wall in shame-filled suicidal despair. I still wonder why I just didn't walk out of the room that day when things got out of control before the memorial service. During the service, I held my mom as she sobbed like I'd never seen her cry, ever. It was such an epic moment to see my mom so real, such a window of relief for me to witness her real feelings. I felt closer to her then than in any other conscious moment of my life. But she hated the experience, which made me feel shame for feeling it was wonderful to see her feel.

My responsibility these days is how I treat my daughters, and the "rough voice," as my four-year-old named it, has gone by the wayside. It raised its ugly mouth when I started overeating again.

I got a strong grip on a let-go attitude and focused my attention on my thinking, attitudes, actions, and behavior toward my daughters, so that ultimately they will not fear me. Anger creates fear and nothing else. My goal is that my daughters will be so unafraid of me that I'm a safe haven for them, if not the safest place in the world, until they inwardly develop their own resting place. If it isn't already intrinsic or instilled in them.

I'm taking a reading break.

I just read a good journal provided by the front office. It's an official guide to my death. Reading it has caused me to think of writing my own obituary, first person, because of my background as a newspaper journalist. Who would be better qualified to write about my life being over than me? It would be kind of a scoop, too, to have a byline after the date of my death, sort of immortalizing me as a writer. Then again, if I just put future dates on my writing and leave it behind, it could be like writing in the future, not just the past or present. But back to the obituary. I'm afraid if I don't write it, someone else will make a mistake in it.

It's all so clear to me what a gift of relief I'm already providing for my girls by establishing my legacy now in this manner of preparation for my death. So far, it has been a huge gift in my life. So why would we not take these actions toward death now, when we know it's inevitable? Why would we want others to plan for us when we could have decided it all ourselves? They might do it wrong. Worse, they might not do it at all. But if it's there and ready, there it is. They almost have to follow your plan, whether they want to or not.

Dying wishes are pretty powerful; people feel highly obligated to grant them. When my former father-in-law wanted a pineapple upside-down cake as his last morsel of food, they didn't bring him cheesecake or no cake. He still had time to ask. But let's say he specified in his will that he wanted cheesecake served at his memorial service. Only a vengeful, resentful child would show up with no cake or chocolate cake just to piss Dad off. People would not be saying, "It's what Dad would have wanted." They'd be saying, "Dad got what he wanted."

Facing death puts life into sharp perspective, but people are usually forced to face it when their lives are at stake rather than willingly, as a hobby. It's much more enjoyable when you can face death when healthy, not unhealthy, and as a special project rather than something to put on the back burner (cremation pun intended). People are only motivated by near-death experiences for a short time, though they may make major life changes after experiencing them. Soon they are back to ignoring death, until the next bout in the hospital. Sorry for the pessimism.

I guess what has motivated me is my chronic near-death experience as a person with bipolar disorder. In retaliation, I've taken chronic and consistent actions over time, which is why I'm so well prepared, to the extreme of writing a book about it. How much nearer to death can you get than sitting four feet from your unmarked grave as your chosen "work?" No one knows I'm doing this, except for the woman from the money program and the woman here whose phone number I took, and they're safe because they're not involved in my daily life. My death community is growing. Dead or alive, we are all living among the dead, the visitors as well as the people they visit. All are part of a neighborhood I'm exploring. Wouldn't it be cool if getting to know my dead neighbors now enables me to see them somehow after I die?

Putting Things in Order says, "If it occurs to you to write your own obituary, you may run the risk of being called a control freak." Gee, that comment will really hurt once I'm dead. Control freaks don't change just because they're called so even when they're alive.

What does this say about the person who actually writes the obituary instead of just thinking about writing it? I've never seen one written in first person, as it should be if you write your own. If you write about yourself in third person, you're a true ghost writer! Mine will be a first-person obituary. I fought long and hard to get front-page newspaper stories. I'll fight hard to get myself in print one last time. Too bad I won't be around to see if it gets published. It will just depend upon how picky the editor is that day and whether he will feel obligated to grant my dying wish. Even then, given the turnover at the office, another boss might not receive my request. "Dear Editor, please grant my wish to run this obituary in the first-person tense. I have a long history in journalism. Thank you for considering publishing my very last story."

I'm finding that the way I face death—or don't—is a direct reflection of how I face life—and don't. What if people who don't face death with honest examination are avoiding life in the same manner? See if that hits home or rings bells. It does for me. Not until I started to work here did I see my huge avoidance of life on all fronts. So, for me, examining death has forced me back into my life, an unexpected journey for certain. Because I thought I was living my life. I didn't know how really dead I was until I arrived here and started writing.

People say death is a part of life, but I prefer to think of it as life being part of death. It's *one*. One state, both of them together. It's one suspended state of consciousness transcending both life and death and basically eliminating distinction. I am here dead as much as I am alive. I don't care if anyone else can "prove" otherwise. Parallel universes, for example, are visible to people who experience them as existing, regardless of what is seen or not seen by others. "Visible" is relative, and "seeing" is more than visual or limited to the sense of sight. A deep knowing causes shifts in the way things are seen; they are viewed with more clarity in dimensions just as real as any other. *Parallel* is even a misnomer. We use that word to describe the unique features of the Oneness or ways of experiencing the elements that make up the Oneness.

I sense all the dead people from my life visiting me here. Whether or not I get to their stories, they come into my thoughts by name and in no particular order as I sit here. With each name comes the presence, and I feel them all surrounding me. Of all of them, Tom was the most alive while living, so it makes sense he's the most alive while dead. He's having the most fun of anybody I know. He's everywhere. I have a feeling my mom will be like that. She loves traveling and has been all over the world. It gives me goose bumps thinking of her exploring the entire cosmos. I wish she could live to tell about it.

In spite of my mom's troubles and challenges, she's always managed to rise above it all and enjoy life ... a lot. Her ability to enjoy her existence, sans troubles and challenges and three dependent adult children and their children, will thrill her to no end. I'm kind of excited for her. Given my perspective, I wonder how hard I'll be crying at her funeral. God forbid I would express any joy. Joy at a funeral looks really bad. You're happy your mother is dead? No one would understand. Let me practice my somber mood and face now so I can get ready for the show. How fake that feels.

I know. I'll do my usual routine when I'm most myself, a

combination of hysterical laughter (joy disguised), even though the volume really bothers my girls, alternating with pure grief in tears that run down my face, with no sound at all. I like the river and raindrops the tears create, so I always say, "No thank you," when someone passes me a tissue. It really bothers people when you don't accept their tissues. Yeah, that's me.

I'm glad I've taken this moment to prepare myself for how to be real at my mother's service. It would be neat to think that my daughters would feel close to me because they saw me being real, even if the laughter annoys them. We all deserve to be annoyed by our mothers and say so out loud, especially to them, without repercussion. It's a child's privilege and normal childhood development.

Putting Things in Order also discusses leaving some money for friends and family to go out after the service for "dinner on me." Think of the relief of not worrying about who picks up the tab in such situations! I think I'll adopt this journal's authors as part of my death community here. Ellen Baumitter and David Finkle. I wonder if they already have their plots. They do have their restaurants picked out. Ellen wants them to go to Chinatown for dim sum and Ferrara's Little Italy for cappuccino and cannoli. (Is this Los Angeles, San Francisco, or New York?) David has a specific, elaborate show planned at a rented hall. I wonder if he already paid for the hall. You can see the show details on page 89 of *Putting Things in Order*.

My children's father and I created our living wills and family trust with an attorney when we first had children. During the divorce, I took him out of mine, a sad task, and formed a trust in my own name. The term living will is perfect for what it stands for; it also rhymes with living well.

Well, I got the call from Mom and decided to take it just for kicks since I'm at our plot and she doesn't know it. Too timely. Her first question was "Where are you?" I had to think fast, because in telling the truth I run the risk of oddity. So I said I was working. How silly. She knows I don't have a "real job." Then she persisted on the *where*, and so I let her in on the name of the city, nervous that I was revealing too much information. She said, "Call back when you can." Since I don't want to talk over my girls later in the day, I said I could take the time now. After all, she is definitely part of this community and this work. She is also my most immediate gravestone neighbor, my permanent neighbor in the afterlife, so I'd better learn to face her. The call went downhill from there.

How many of you get off the phone after talking with your mother and shake? I've seen my own voice affect my children that way in person. We got into it over me not calling her back ... again. You'd think I'd just learn to call her back right away to avoid the issue. But no. She's onto my isolation, and she's one of those psychic moms who always knows when something's amiss. By the end of our cemetery conversation, I did apologize for any misunderstandings she might have suffered. It's so sad to me that our first cemetery conversation was a disaster. It may have been the only live grave-site talk we'll ever have. Well, at least it was honest, because this is how it is on occasion. Can't fake it from the grave. I'm sure once we are both buried here we'll get along famously and never have a harsh or misunderstood or missing word. And there will be no more phone-call expectations.

Back to living well. Tomorrow would be a good day to have lunch with Mom. I told her, "I think the girls will bring you joy." I can't live well if I'm afraid of my mother, so facing her will be good for me. And we won't have time again until her birthday in six weeks.

I have to leave to pick up the girls and take them home. I already know I will be in trouble. I have taken a big hit by engaging the way I did with Mom, which set me up for agitation in my own mothering. What can I do to ward it off, to dissolve it? Anger between my mother and me disables my own mothering. I hung up feeling guilty, and this demands excessive quantities of food as payback.

The conversation replays in my head. It's too late. The chemical reaction took hold, and now I want to go binge. And I'm afraid to pick up my girls. And I beat myself up for how I get crippled by giving other people the power to affect the course of my living well, even though it's really me using them to cripple myself. Make sense?

What would living well look like today? Maybe living well isn't orchestrating the day but listening to the orchestra. I'll try to just show up, listen, and be guided. This time, I will report back about how the experiment went. I have a feeling already that I will write "it went well," due to my skillful time-traveling thought process, along with the ferocious desire I have to live—and live well—this day.

Three Days Later

It's true. I can't write this book anywhere but here. I tried again last night, and the words didn't come. Despite that failure, I still think that by the end of this book I'll take my resting place home.

Quail live here? This is not the desert, but I just saw one.

This morning I want to write about my daughters.

I started a journal about each daughter. These are separate from the journals containing the letters I've written to them twice a year since pregnancy. The new journals are for meditating upon my girls on an ongoing basis. I behold them in my heart and try to get a vision of their spirits, focusing on what they might need from the day and what they might need from me. Then I jot down in the journals the thoughts that occur to me. This method of meditative parenting needs to go in my *Soul Custody* book. The way it exercises my heart muscle, I really feel it.

I forgot the Deep Woods spray, and I'll have four hours here, having skipped yoga and the gym for this spiritual workout, the longest stretch yet, because I was so excited to visit my grave this morning.

I love my daughters more than any other human beings, and I love them equally for who they are. Such fairness in distribution of love does not mean they equally feel the expression of such love. Quirks in my personality, fear, over-identification, and projection can ruin my ability to express love to any of them at any given time. But the basic loving, supportive foundation is there. Ultimately, the love they feel from me depends on their own unique ability to interpret and internalize it.

When I take my girls to see Grandma, I observe the fruits of Mom's attempts and my attempts at a better life for our collective children. Mom did better with me than her mom did with her. I do better with my girls than my mom did with me. They'll do better with their children than I did with them. We're all doing the best we can.

I'm still bothered by the absence of mother-daughter grave combos here. I reviewed the rules, and there really aren't any, other than flowers and plants needing to be in their own containers. I just don't want to break the rules. That's how I am in life, so careful not to do anything wrong to protect my already too-deep well of shame. Growing up with too much shame at the core of my being is the source of my suicidal chemical streak. I'm doubtful it represents my true nature, but I do feel it's too formidable in constitution to let my true nature win out in this lifetime. I've accepted it as part of the chemical makeup of my brain. How it's wired. Perhaps my spirit has a shame infection that is incurable.

Who cares, really, how I got it? Ultimately, the issue is how to survive it. I would be more likely to die from existing conditions, mental illness to the point of overeating that leads to a fatal condition, or alcoholism causing an accident or severely damaging my health. Those are my "cancers," and no others have been added to the list.

I'm sad this morning. On the same day in 1992, I experienced the happiest day of my life, my wedding day. I only managed to acknowledge it in a feeble, under-serving voicemail message I left for a friend who didn't even like him. "I'm feeling loss of my love for him getting to be expressed." So even though I saw him yesterday, it didn't occur to me to say something about August 19, 1992. This heaped on more sadness and triggered the additional loss of not knowing what words might have been appropriate. It felt dishonoring to the day to remain silent with my girls about it.

This became mixed up with the desire to refrain from doing anything unhealthy in the way of romantic tricks that would start to stir up something dishonest, selfish, or fear based, given that he is now taken. So I didn't trust myself. I just let out the grief, lying back on my staircase, realizing no one could save me from it or feel it for me. That's okay. August 19 is no less important just because I didn't do it justice today. Also, string theory to the rescue: today is that day, still. So no loss. It's actually still part of the Great Reality of Right Now. Tears ended. Tears are probably more from the lack of recognition of that fact than anything else.

The connection, however it is with him today—unspoken, parental—is what it needs to be, cultivated by mutual care for our girls. That connection is the most important after a marriage with children ends. So I lucked out.

While there's time, what else do I want to do, to get to know, to experience? I hope I gain a larger perspective on those choices by the end. I hope if I ever do meet and marry the good doctor that I don't brag about marrying again as some proof that I'm not a failure. I'm expected to want a relationship. Cousin's husband asks, "Are you dating anyone?" Next time he asks, I'll say, "Could you stop asking me that? I promise you'll be the first to know."

I wonder if I really don't want a relationship, and I am the last to know. Oh, it's already occurring. I forgot. Yes, highest consciousness has unlimited capacity. It's my low state of consciousness that would claim there's no room for love in my life. It's already there; I'm just not consciously aware of it, just as he is still here, as clear as he was on August 19. My awareness is of a dead relationship, when all that ever was is really all very much alive.

As I write here, I am getting cramped up in my upper body. I wore my leather fur coat to be cozy in my internal world, but after an hour hunched over while scrawling intensely and exploring my interior life deeply, my body aches from the exercise.

I'm now going to turn to the list of things I wanted to address in this book. Random issues left untouched, undone.

My children's father accidentally found his mother's plot here when he was taking a psychology class at a local medical institution. Back in the early 1960s, his father had donated her body to science as she'd wished. The teacher informed him that in those days, bodies donated to science in Southern California went to the medical center. He looked her up and, sure enough, there was her name. The Gateway staff took him to the unmarked grave where 200 bodies donated to science, including hers, were buried. So that year, as a Christmas present, I bought a marker for her resting place for $750. We dedicated it to the bodies of science and put her name at the bottom. Finally, forty years after her death, my husband found his mom by accident.

I wonder why the neighboring little girl's parents don't call; wouldn't they want her memorialized in a book?

Back to the list.

I forgot to mention *Wrong Number*, that comedy for the big screen. Premise: What if we said, "Hello, who are you; how can I help you?" in response to every wrong number called or received instead of hanging up on them? A kind of Jim Carrey *Yes Man* film. I need collaborators. And Jim Carrey to star in it, as long as I write it before he gets too old for the role or dies.

That brings up a good point for examination. In spite of my friendly disposition, I do not feel I get close enough to people. You'd never know I have this difficulty with people unless you were the other person and noticed. Most don't notice. My mother and I agree we are not in love with people, but she loves humanity, while I do not. I love the spirit within humanity but not the human condition, human nature, human needs, or what it means to be human.

I don't like it that my daughters' lives are subject to all things human, including death. I love those three human beings more than I love myself, which is why I stay alive for them, even though I know I'm supposed to love myself first and most. My daughters transcend humanity, which may not be the best perspective for me to have as their mother. I wouldn't want to infect them with my difficulty with (and about) the human condition. This really must come from my alcoholism, though I'm sober. Recovery literature describes alcoholism as an inability to form true partnerships with others. I prefer Spirit.

I don't even really like breathing. It's too hard to get a full breath. I don't like what it means to be alive. Is it because my spirit is suffocated in this body? Am I despairing? Is something wrong with me, because I don't want to be here? Or is it just the acceptable truth of my life? I wish I could be here for my daughters and dead at the same time. Meaning, I wish I could just live for my daughters and nothing else, be nothing else, and focus on nothing else. I'm tired. Life in all other arenas is too hard for me. I've been through too much for my psyche to handle any more "life," regardless of whether external situations warrant this state of mind or not.

What would happen if I let all the rest go in favor of just paying attention to love in my heart, home, and writing? Let all else fade or fall away, including my obsessive definitions of work, friendships, and activities, taking responsibility only for what is before me in any given moment? This will be my experiment for today. How frightening a prospect. It sounds tragically bleak and morose as I write it.

I've been here two hours and am more than halfway done with work. Here comes a golf cart to tell me I've outworn my welcome.

How typical that I don't feel I deserve to be anywhere, not even my grave. After I die, I'll probably still check in at the office to ask, "Is it okay that I'm still here? Is there a curfew? Are you sure I'm not taking up too much of your time? Excuse me, do I deserve to live?" And then, "Do I deserve to die?" No wonder I need a resting place. I'm cultivating a place I feel I deserve, because I don't feel deserving of life or death.

I do feel deserving of occupying the space in this blank book, and that's why I have a chronic desperation to fill it up. To be here consistently. Deep down, then, I must feel worthy of having a voice, because I want to publish this. I must feel deserving of having a voice in the world.

The golf cart carried two ladies from the office. I can't help thinking they are really spying on me but remaining perfectly, respectfully distant and quiet, pretending to survey plots by number. By the way, I want to find out what my number is. I won't be a social security number anymore. I'll be a plot number. I should memorize it.

Did I mention I'm far more comfortable around the dead than the living? For example, I'm perfectly happy with my death-long neighbors. But when I tried to find relatives yesterday, it was terrifying, and I'm glad my phone calls met a dead end. The phone book included only a last name matching a pharmacy in Fontana. They didn't know the name but sent me to corporate, which returned me to the pharmacy. I could do an Internet search, use Facebook, or call 411. But I realized I prefer my feeble attempt and dead end to actually finding the living.

What would I say if I reached someone? "Hi, I'm your mom's neighbor up here at Gateway. I've always wanted to meet you." Maybe I can give up the ghost on that effort. Why do I push myself out there so much when it isn't what I like or want? I'm constantly trying to deny that I'm really antisocial. Maybe I'm trying to deny the Great Reality I'm already connected with forever.

I enjoy the persona of the reclusive manic depressives who can't get along with people but are brilliant. I indulge in such identification and self-pity. The only part I don't like is not producing a work of art, as most of them do. Nothing horrifies me more than thinking of the hours I've lived inside this journal and fearing that no one will ever find me, see it, and read it, because I'm a disturbed manic depressive who thinks I've got a best seller when really it's unoriginal, nothing new or worthwhile, nothing anyone wants to read, let alone buy, publish, distribute, and put in bookstores. To counter this horror, I vow to die trying.

To get to the end of life without one creative body of work put out there? I have to stay alive just to prevent that. I don't like the idea of posthumous fame, because they might find something I didn't get to edit.

Back to my notes. It's important to keep up with my notes as I go along, because I want the process to keep moving forward.

You know what's worse than being homeless in this world? Being lifeless. In the film *Braveheart*, Mel Gibson says, "Everybody dies, but not every man really lives." He's talking about freedom making us truly alive. I would imagine freedom means different things to different people. For me, it's the freedom to choose how to live. I have a home, but I feel lifeless because I feel closer to death than to life. It's not due to ingratitude, and it's separate from the love I feel for my girls and the need to be there for them. As I wrote earlier, I have trouble drawing a breath and feel my *life-less-ness* means my spirit is about to be extinguished.

I'm caught up with my notes now and feel agitated. Maybe this is my writing limit. But I doubt it. I still have to write my way to the end of this book so I can close it and take my first deep breath.

My resting place is where my spirit is entering my body again. The way it inhabited it before. That's probably why I wanted to take dancing lessons yesterday. How ironic to come here wanting to crawl under the headstone and leave here having crawled back into my body. How easy it is to return. Automatic. I just breathe. Re-spirit myself. *Respirate.* Take a breath. Then make it safe around me, safe to breathe. Create safety, whatever that means for me in the environment, like no mean people. I've been doing that naturally to keep from overeating. Eating made my environment feel safe. Who cares how or why it happened; it just did. As long as I had food around me and weight, it buffered any harshness in the environment. I have to enforce the safety rules now instead of abdicating the job to Starbucks or Häagen Dazs.

I'm so glad I don't have to water Mom's yellow silk flower. I hate watering plants.

Back to the original question this morning: While there's time, what else do I want to do, to get to know, to experience? It's clear that I'm a narrow-minded, small-visioned human who lacks perspective and has no clue about my potential abundant choices. I have no idea of all that is available to me that I don't avail myself of. This is part of lifelessness. Not seeing beyond my home. In the grand scheme, which I can't see, I'm not aware of my choices or how to select them or how to live my way into them. How can I when I don't know they're there? This includes where to travel, what to write, how to bring something of value into the world in addition to children, and how to participate in cyberspace. This extends to all the same possibilities and potentials for my children that I'm not tapped into.

At the same time, I ignore everything historical that I have in the garage, the experience and life treasures accumulated, the writing trail I left behind me, the resources collected. I blind myself to the Great Unknown of my own life, my self-interior, the world at large, the spiritual realm, and ultimately everything I already have and am, conscious and unconscious. Choices paralyze me.

I suppose it will become simpler once I discover the results of my experiment to make decisions based on heart, with daughters and journals at the core.

That reminds me of something I must decide. I have to determine which journals to be buried with, which to leave behind, and which to destroy. I want to know ahead of time every word

I've left behind. *I've got it!* I want to be buried with one blank journal or a journal I choose ahead of time, so I will know about it. Blanks are my favorite. But that's wasting paper, since it isn't recycling. Blank pages? Let me think on that some more.

Maybe there's a written journal I'll take with me. I archived my journal writing collection in 2003. Weeding out half my collection took a year. But there's more work to do on the collection so that it isn't so unwieldy or cumbersome for whoever gets to keep it. Yes, I tried to turn the process into a book. It's still unfinished. I created a workshop called "Pandora's Box: Managing a Private Journal Collection." It's a great deal of fun.

It isn't what I have yet to experience. It's a matter of which experiences I have had that I want to revisit, assimilate, and bring into today in some interpretive way. This includes photographs. The writing and memorabilia are all scattered like disassembled puzzle pieces, and I want to collect them, put them together in some fashion, and only then build on the puzzle. This simply involves taking a look and deciding where to put things, holding and examining what I have in my possession. Another "Fall Harvest" after my "Fruits of Summer." I give all my journals cute titles.

Yes, I want to do a home inventory. Assemble the puzzle pieces of my life, which include my journal collection, so that everything tells a story of who I am. Those are the places I want to go. The places I've been. Bring the past to the present and live my string theory. I don't even know if string theory has anything to do with past, present, and future all being one, but that's what I'm referring to and the vocabulary I use. This perspective gives me a better ability to come to greater awareness of all things. Because I ignore/negate/leave behind this conscious awareness of all that has been, I lose touch with the now that contains so much more. So it's critical to bring it all forward.

While it could be viewed as going *back* over my life, it's really *sideways*. Think parallel. Moving in and out of the experiences that make up the full picture, moving forward by advancing in conscious awareness. Not literally getting on with life by leaving things behind or moving on. If we are with everything all the time, there's no leaving behind or moving on from any of it.

This is my favorite spot in the entire world. Probably because it's my only spot, the portal through which I'm allowing my spirit to flow back into my body as I breathe and write here.

Odd. I thought the answer to "while there's time" would be a bucket list. Maybe the answer is in "while there's timelessness." We created time to order our lives and mark how we live, and how well we live. I have some work to do that can't be bothered by active addictions.

How good it feels to write my heart out. What good spiritual exercise. It's amazing how four hours feels like an instant. How timeless everything really is. I've been asking the wrong questions. I've been wrong in asking questions of life and of my life.

It's time to fully try on new perspectives that emerge fully on their own. I root my day now in meditation to allow life to grow in consciousness that day, this day, which is every day. One big, huge cycle of everything coordinating and operating simultaneously, a constant state of randomness, possibility, options, choices. It would be great to think, feel, and know I cannot go wrong, but I don't feel that directed yet. I'm barely breathing.

More than half my journal is written. I'll be back here tomorrow and Monday.

The Next Day

I had a major panic attack on the way to work here this morning. It took four phone calls, a thirty-minute walk, and prayer. Some days you just don't want to go to work. The panic resulted from the fun I had here yesterday. I wrote for four hours straight, hunched over in my rock chair, with arm cramping and hand and shoulder straining, because I finally rolled up my sleeves to get down and dig in the dirt.

Naturally, I wanted to return today, only now I have all day to write. I decided to stay here eight hours, with a lunch break, to make it my first full-time day of work as a writer.

I recall that at some point when I was under the age of ten, I wanted to write a book. Key word *write*. Notice that I didn't dream of publishing a book. My dream was to write one. So my dream has already transpired. I'm definitely writing a book.

I've arrived at work disheveled and mismatched, wearing last night's makeup. I forgot to bring the paperwork from the cemetery office that I planned to bring today, and I forgot bug repellent. *Why don't they make bee repellent?* Part of me loves this rawness and imperfection once I'm in the flow of things. The soul thrives on chores, including laundry. So it must like dirty clothes; otherwise it wouldn't so enjoy washing them.

At my Sunday meeting earlier this morning, my writer friend Elizabeth shared about losing a lifelong friend to one of those massive out-of-the-blue heart attacks that strike healthy people. She looked straight at me, with tears trickling down her face. As if somehow she knew I was on my way to my resting place, she said, "Why do we place so much emphasis on our bodies? They're just shells!"

I was stunned. Should I be thinking more about where my spirit will be or go than where my shell ends up? Why such an emphasis on this speck of dirt just large enough for an urn under a granite slab? Is that the element my marker is made of? Where will I be? Everywhere, indeed. However, that presupposes that only after death are we everywhere. What if we are everywhere already? What if our spirits are everywhere and inhabiting the shell at the same time? In that case, what is the shell for?

Why can't we all just be one happy *One* together. One spirit, one body? Why are our spirits contained in shells? Maybe they aren't shells that contain spirits but rather spirits that contain shells, a manifestation of spirit, like water, a rock, or a tree. And what does this mean for everyday living?

Are answers to these questions even necessary? I asked my friend Robin why God gave us free will if he knew we would blow it, make mistakes, harm each other, and make a mess of the world. In her wisdom, she said people have been asking that question for all time. What if the answers don't come because they're the wrong questions ... or unnecessary questions? We do live according to how we believe.

By the way, overnight I came to believe I do have friends. They're starting to come into focus again.

Back to the panic attack. It also stemmed from an insight shared by a woman at the eating disorder meetings I attend. She said if she doesn't do something creative, she's at risk for overeating. Deep down I know if I don't write as my heart speaks, the food will tattle on me that I'm not putting in an authentic and honest day's work. It's a betrayal of the heart to do work contrary to a calling.

John had me identify the mission behind what I really want to do in life. In other words, what is the driving force behind the books I want to write? I was surprised to discover that I want to help people see things from different perspectives. This focus allows me to bring forth an originality and authenticity no one else has or can duplicate. That's what I meant by doing an honest day's work. I'm being who I really am.

There's a lot of work to be done here today. I've rolled up my sleeves and started digging with my pen. I intend to plan my memorial service, finish my notes, and end the book, leaving several pages blank. That's because, as of last night, my four-year-old daughter provided its conclusion. More on that later. I'm on a roll.

To brave the drive up the main road, I blasted U2's "Where The Streets Have No Name." No wonder I like this song. "I want to run. I want to hide. I want to tear down the walls that hold me inside." In my case this morning, those walls are my casket, a cubicle I work in. This book will help me live out of the box. I've already opened the lid, and I sat up to look around.

I'm freezing. I'm glad I brought the leather fur coat. There, all cozy now. Better take care of the shell. It contains the spirit.

I took my girls out to dinner last night, and everyone was a bit cranky. My youngest wouldn't sit in her chair, the service was slow, and they didn't bring us any water. I was rushed, as I needed to get to a meeting on time, which made me impatient. As I obsessed over whether to have chicken or salmon, two of the girls started arguing over what one of them said to the other and complaining about not getting a booth, all the normal irritations of a luxury existence. Meanwhile, my littlest crawled into my lap and said she wanted to *rest*. The word caught my attention. Suddenly, Mom's mood changed. Because that's contagious, the other girls started playing a game with the crayons. I felt like I was holding my youngest as a newborn baby, with the same amount of love at first sight. I asked her, "Is this your resting place?" She looked straight at me with all the earnestness and preciousness of a four-year-old and said, "Mommies are the best resting places."

Oh, my God. Do you get it? I am The Resting Place. It is not a place I go to or create, bring, or take. It's something I *am*! Think of it. Our babies rest in our wombs, except when they're kicking us. We rest in our mother's arms, if we're lucky. We rest our heads on their chests. We rest on them and listen to their heartbeats or voices until we fall asleep. Some of us get to rest, even sleep, next to our mothers for a time. We try all our lives to put any unrest with our mothers to rest. And one day, we put our mommies to rest. It's natural to want to come to a resting place with them. Although our fathers plant the seeds, we grow in our mothers' bodies, their shells, which means that they are the human beings closest to us, whether we grow up knowing them or not. If I'm not mistaken, Mother's Day is a far more emotionally charged holiday than Father's Day.

Here comes the golf cart again. Aren't they ever going to ask me why I come here for days on end, spending hours at a time, or ask what I'm writing? I wonder what I look like on the surveillance camera. I try to keep my clothes on and avoid spontaneous dancing, blasting my car stereo, or picking my nose. I even tone down any silly dance I do when trying to get away from those bees.

Oh, it isn't a golf cart. It's a mom. I can't break the code of silence by asking her questions. She's a resting place; that's all I need to know. Same for my neighbors here. But what about the three-year-old? And what about women who don't have children? Well, the little girl had a mom, a resting place. Women who don't have children also have moms, so just by virtue of association, they are resting places. The evidence of that is the love a mother feels for her child, regardless of how that child treats her. Even if she doesn't feel it, that great love still exists in potential in a parallel universe, a hidden dimension, of which the mother is unaware.

Since fathers make mothers mothers, would they be resting places by association? Are we all human resting places? All I know is that it's perfect now that I'm next to my mom here, and I was right to combine being closest to her via birth with being closest to her via death.

So my conclusion is that the shell is a resting place. The shell, containing the beating heart, is a manifestation of spirit. This may not be news to you, but it is for me. It goes with me wherever I go. I cannot not be at my resting place, because it is within me. I think my spirit is resting here for a time, just resting. My spirit is greater than my shell, yes, but it takes great effort to bring this to consciousness and see how both are possible simultaneously. You'll have to read my forthcoming book on the

Theory of Everything for that.

When I leave here, I won't write at some other resting place. I'll write from my resting place within. I'm so excited to do my first entry at home. Now it will seem natural; I just know it. I feel as if I've been laid to rest, raised from the dead, immortalized, resuscitated, and respirated. I've been liberated spiritually, physically, emotionally, and mentally. I'm back from the dead.

I wonder how many dead people are walking around in life like I was? Maybe I should be on the lookout for them. What could I do to help bring them back to life? Well, if I am a resting place, perhaps I will feel like that to anyone who notices, maybe even to those with death wishes like mine. Maybe living fully is a contagious cure. I'll find out.

What about my memorial service? Someone once told me that we have grieving all backward. We should cry at births and rejoice at deaths. How true. We come into our shells and endure an existence, trying our entire lives to find a resting place that may only be found after we die. But if we were to discover The Resting Place before death ... wow, imagine the possibilities. We live forever now, while alive. We go everywhere here, now. We're part of the One, and also separate human beings. Most importantly, we rest in our bodies. And maybe once we're at rest, we take better care of our bodies.

Okay, so I want to throw a party for my memorial service. Let me think out of the box. When I was thirty-six, I had a bikini party in the park. How about a dance this time? They can say, "She always wanted to dance but never did. Now she can." Perhaps this explains why out of the blue on Friday, as my youngest was in ballet class, I secretly decided to use the coupon that I'd stashed away a year ago for a free class. I know the good

doctor dances. But I don't want to be a divorcee who takes dancing lessons, similar to Richard Gere in the film *Shall We Dance*,
with Jennifer Lopez and Susan Sarandon. I don't like the idea of
holding hands and touching moving bodies. But, well, they are
just shells. And if my spirit is everywhere, then I can get close to
people. And if it's true that we're One in consciousness, then I'm
already as close as one can get. So I may as well dance.

I want to have a dance with music that will suit all ages. A mix.
What if friends and relatives are shy, offended, or embarrassed
to dance at a memorial? My girls would be mortified (except for
the youngest). Well, then, they can stay home and visit my plot
all somber some other time. I don't mind. Whatever they need to
do to be true to themselves. But I love watching my girls dance,
so let us dance. They get to pick some of the songs. I'll have a
few selected in advance.

Some songs won't be danceable, such as "Somewhere in Time,"
an instrumental by John Barry. I'd also like an instrumental version of "Beautiful Dreamer," which would be too hard for anyone
to find if I don't locate it first. *Oh, wait!* I have a music box that
plays it! Someone can just open the lid. A DJ can take requests,
too. I would love it if my sister and her husband would show
everyone their Viennese waltz, as they did on their wedding day
in 1990. Maybe my ballerina daughter could do a solo to a Nut-
cracker song. And perhaps Van Morrison's "Someone Like You,"
my August 19 wedding song, could be played for *him*. All this
sounds so weird, and none of it goes together.

But, oh, it will be heavenly! I'm looking at the spot for it right
now. It might be a little small under a tent. But if we put up two
tents, people could just dance barefoot on the grass. I don't want
to be so controlling that I force people to do things that make
them feel awkward. On the other hand, if they secretly want to

dance barefoot but are just inhibited, my final wishes will give them the permission they need. Take my invisible hand, let me lead you to the dance floor, and watch where you step in this place.

I'd like anyone who wants to speak or read something to have a voice before the dance. All friends, family, and acquaintances will be welcome. It could be open to the public for those who don't know me, too, but by RSVP only, because the cemetery space is limited in the garden district. I know there are some people who just like to go to people's funerals, even if they don't know them. Is that legal?

I'll find the DJ I want and look at the suggestions and guidelines offered by the Gateway planners.

I will write something for someone to read. I want to address the crowd and certain people individually in front of the group. I want to have a blank journal ready for people to write in as a keepsake for my girls, and I won't call it "Parting Thoughts." We aren't apart and not parting. I'll get back to you on the actual title.

White roses. No balloons, please. There are enough of those on the main street through here, which I call Mylar Boulevard.

I really don't want any photographs displayed unless I find one or two that I like in my garage treasure hunt as I collect my life this fall.

Ideally, I'd get everyone up at 4:00 a.m. for the memorial, but they'd never forgive me. Or it would be a no-show. But I do want everything to happen only in the morning hours.

I want my resting place pointed out and to have already been cremated and laid to rest there, with the words engraved on my marker so people can see exactly where they can visit me anytime they don't feel me with them in spirit. They'll know right where to find me.

I don't want to plan where they go to eat afterward. I purchased too much food in this life already. It's that simple. Specifics will follow.

A guest list to a memorial service seems a bit overboard, don't you think? But who knows who I know and how to reach them? If I were to die today, there's no one who knows how to locate my friends. No one will want to spend time searching when they're grieving. I'd better make a list of the people to contact. When I gave birth to my daughters, I handed over the birth plan, and that included a list of people to contact. Same thing with my memorial service.

That's all I can think of for my service, except that I don't call it a celebration of life because I want to give memorial services a new spin. I think it should be called a celebration of death. It's okay to celebrate death ... not only okay but accurate. I feel like Woody Allen, who said, "I don't believe in the afterlife, but I am bringing a change of underwear."

Today I'm taking the yellow rose and evergreen candle home. Neither of our shells are here yet. But my very first resting place is now my last.

I have never seen a bee eat a fly, but that's just what one is doing next to me. I'm not afraid, sitting a foot away, because he's on a mission and oblivious to me. My fear of bees is so ironic, since my name in Greek means "all honey." I'm terrified of bees and yet they make what I am. They love me, so maybe this means I'm terrified of myself.

I think I mentioned the possibility of having to plan Mom's memorial first. I need to discover her favorite song. I already know her favorite flower; she loves ranunculus the most. I don't think I've ever seen one. If I have, I didn't know that's what it was. She'd better die when they're in season, or maybe I can find silk or plastic versions. Of course, I have the poem she wrote in high school that was published in the school journal.

I want to have a service for her here under the tent. Unveil her plot with the name already on it. I have the one picture of her, a beautiful portrait I had taken as a birthday present. And I'll have to have an art show at a gallery in Redlands. It will be necessary to plan it ahead of time so I can find one worthy of and agreeable to such a thing. I'd call it the Mary Moore Gallery Memorial Art Exhibit. Maybe it should be in La Jolla, because that's where she had her gallery in the 1970s. It would be open to the public the afternoon of the service. With a break for lunch. Then the art show in Redlands.

For Dad, I only want to do one thing: Read Emerson's quote on success, which Dad loves. I don't think he likes music; I can't think of a single song he's ever mentioned. I'll read the quote. There isn't anything I care to say, because we have said it all while alive. I'd prefer to honor him in perfect peace and quiet. If he hasn't accomplished his lifelong dream to see his pet project, "Save Our Stories," see the light of day, the privilege of seeing that dream through will be my inheritance.

Here's the quote for Dad:

> To laugh often and much; to win the respect of intelligent people and the affection of children; to earn the appreciation of honest critics and endure the betrayal of false friends; to appreciate the beauty; to find the best in others; to leave the world a bit better, whether by a healthy child, a garden patch, or a redeemed social condition; to know even one life has breathed

easier because you have lived. This is to have succeeded.
— *Attributed to Ralph Waldo Emerson (1803–1882)*

I'll have to be really careful how I eat after he dies. My eating disorder is linked to Dad in ways I can't express or identify. I just know the unconscious forces lurk there, ready to unfurl. Especially when you add grief to the recipe.

I've never thought about what I'd do at my stepmother's memorial service. We've never talked about it. She probably has hers planned anyway, as I do. She's like that. Maybe I'll ask her what she would want me to read. There is a long piece she wrote for a second memorial service we had for Tom called "One Family." I'll dig it up from archived emails, print it out, and evaluate. I want to read something she wrote. She was a prolific and unpublished author, so it's only fair. She was a newspaper reporter in the day, but it will probably fall to me to publish posthumously her epic 600+ page book *Half Souls.*

Of course, I could borrow from what I did for her mother's memorial service, who was my step-grandmother, Lila Mohr. That side of the family is linked to Joseph Mohr, who wrote the words to "Silent Night" in poem form before it became the Christmas carol with lyrics by Franz Gruber. So at Lila's service, I recited "Silent Night" like a poem. The reason this wouldn't do justice to my stepmother is that she is such a fabulous poet and writer herself, better than Joseph. But she never published her work beyond poetry she wrote as a child and her journalism as an adult, which included being selected as a Pulitzer Prize finalist. I haven't spoken with her recently about any bucket list she might have at home. In fact, I now recall she and my father saying they plan to be buried in Bisbee, Arizona, with her parents, the "Silent Night" ancestors. Shows you how even when families do discuss things, they're forgotten unless on paper.

If my children's father dies before me without having planned his services, I will read his poetry. A collection of his writings is also unpublished to date but worthy of Barnes and Noble's best-seller section for sure. If he could just gather everything he's written and finish that great novel he started twenty years ago before he dies ... I was riveted by the three pages he did finish. Maybe I'll ask him what poem he would want me to read especially for our daughters, who will be there. Afterward, his reception will feature wall-to-wall displays of his epic journalistic history. And people, including me, will get up to tell stories about him. He will always be my favorite journalist of all time.

I'm genuinely sad now. What's going on? I care about people deeply. I care about them so much my heart hurts, and I cry. I cry because I care about them, not that they're gone or could be gone. Why caring is so painful, I'll never understand. One good thing about overeating is that if you do it enough you could care less about anyone other than the people who serve up your binge foods and the hours they're working. But even then we think of the product rather than the people who provide it for us. They're just the drug dealers, and the drug they provide is legal. I don't recall the name tag of any person from whom I ever bought a binge food.

I don't want to leave here today with the thought that this is my last entry for this book. I know I can come here anytime, and I will. But I'll arrive with a fresh, blank book and without a death wish. I don't want to leave here today, because I'll be out of the box and among the living, out of my comfort zone, disoriented without my death wish. It is just easier to stay closer to death than to life, and I know I'm not alone in that.

On my children's father's birthday last Sunday I emailed him that I'd placed a flower on his mom's grave. I told him I had the feeling she would be proud of us as parents and approve of his lady friend, who looks like her, by the way. His mother's plot is situated right along Mylar Boulevard, against the curb on the right. Hers is the last marker on the left of the row of bodies for science. It reads "Loving Mother —Red Cross Nurse." Below that are the dates the interred bodies passed, between 1965 and 1968. Of the 200 other people buried in the same spot, only my former husband's mother has relatives who know there is a grave with a marker in their memory. Think of all the friends I could make if I contacted those other families.

Resting Place is such a good name. It rhymes with rest in peace, RIP. If you take out the middle letter, you have RP, the initials of Resting Place.

Don't let anyone kid you. Death is really funny if you let it be. The very fact that it's so comical is part of the celebration of life. That information would be good for any memorial service. I'll tell you a funny story about Devon, the girl my father and stepmother unofficially adopted. She pulled the plug on herself in 1993 when her spirit wearied of cystic fibrosis ten years past her life expectancy. She had a morbid fascination with death. *Harold and Maude* was her favorite movie. She was very funny, but we never really joked around. I wish we had. She found humor in death long before I did, probably because she lived so close to it.

The story doesn't seem so funny now. What was the funny story? My stepmother knows them all, but I can't recite even one.

Wow, there's a lot of work left to be done, according to my notes. But it's time for lunch. I'll eat here.

The truth is, I'm never going to get away from food. It's going to chase me into the grave. To stay alive, I have to eat. I don't have to drink alcohol, but I do have to drink water. It's the same with food. I don't have to eat the foods that kill, but I do have to eat what will keep me alive. I kept myself inside the box by believing I could write only if I didn't overeat. And it's true that I do lose my voice when I shove the food in. But look what Oprah does for the literary world, and she openly admits her food issues are ongoing. Well, there goes my theory that I'm only worthy when refraining from all addictions.

The question is, all things being equal, who will race to the grave first with this disease? If it is, indeed, the killer in the end? Does she who has the most books published win? "Skinny people die, too," says the 400-pound binger. I don't want to fool myself that life depends on abstinence, but I'd be a fool to ignore that I increase my fatality potential by overeating.

Now for some humor.

"She has a death wish," our psychotherapist told my boyfriend in 1989 after a couple's therapy session. How did he know? He'd only met me once before, when I accompanied my boyfriend to his therapy session. What did I let slip by accident? Was he trying to warn him not to marry me? More to the point, so what if I do? It didn't stop him from marrying me. It probably sealed the proposal for someone who'd lost his mom as a boy, given how we gravitate to the familiar. It didn't stop us from divorcing either, but that's beside the point. He spent twenty years with me in spite of my death wish, and I'm very proud of that accomplishment. I'm proud, as well, that I've succeeded at staying alive. My death wish also didn't stop him from having three daughters with me and one miscarriage that we know of. All of us are very much alive, except for the one who didn't make it.

Let me tell you about my death wish. I'll be dead honest about it. No one wants to be dead honest while alive, which is why they call it *dead* honest. Through my skillful overeating, my death wish has been fulfilled while I'm still alive. Speaking of food, in spite of previous attempts, I only stopped overeating at 11:59 p.m. on August 3, 2011. I've had periodic problems since I started writing this book. But on August 4, I wrote something from my resting place and discovered that I don't really want to die. I just feel undeserving of living fully. There's a difference.

Earlier in my life, I felt I could push the boundaries of this physical world with greater confidence. One of the craziest things I ever did, thankfully when sober, was to get in my mother's 1981 Blue Honda Accord LX at age fifteen. It was just after my first love taught me how to drive over the telephone so I could go to his house in the middle of the night. Mom intended that car to be a gift for my sixteenth birthday, and I hadn't even taken driver's ed. "Just put it in R to back up, D to go forward, and stay between the yellow lines," said the boy who is now a member of the California Highway Patrol.

I made it from La Jolla to Rancho Bernardo twenty minutes up Interstate 15 and even made it home alive by 4:00 a.m. But it had rained, and a wet car wouldn't make sense to my mother in the morning, as it should have been sitting in its spot inside the parking garage all night. So I took off my clothes, dried the car, put my wet clothes on, and snuck upstairs. I told her this story not long ago. My point is that I miss that teenage feeling of invincibility. And, by the way, don't try this at home. But if you do, be sure to call the California Highway Patrol for the perfect escort.

I'd like to stay alive past December of 2012 just to witness whatever widespread panic an apocalypse creates, and I have a lot of earthquake preparedness to continue doing in the mean-time. This book is so timely, especially if we're all going together next winter. If we go together, I would have wasted ten grand on this plot; maybe I should have taken the girls on a trip with that money. But I can't do everything before December of 2012. That only leaves me sixteen months to collect my life, write three books, and make two movies, all of which will enjoy a very brief shelf life, if any, before the deadline. But just as life is a journey, not a destination, death is a journey, a process, not a deadline.

So everything I've written here still applies. I'll have my rest-ing place now and my resting place after 2012. I wonder where my shell would end up in a catastrophic earthquake? Hopefully it will pass without a sound, like Y2K. I think what is meant to happen by December of 2012 is the end of a certain conscious-ness in humankind and the emergence of a new one. I'll be on the lookout for it in myself.

So the answer, still, is to get to work among the living. I can't die yet. I have so much more work to do. Look at all this Gate-way paperwork on planning. Who are these people who plan fully? I want to meet them. The Gateway planners should hold a social, a mixer for planners to network, share ideas, and get to know one another before their afterlife solidarity in the cem-etery. Meanwhile, I have to go back to college just to learn the planning software offered for sale in the office. I need to get updated on computer technology so I won't die outdated.

Some people make films to present at their services! You should see the possibilities for posterity! As a film major in col-lege who still hasn't produced a film, I would fear such a movie would be my one and only. Well, I didn't really want to make films when I signed up for a film degree at San Diego State Uni-versity. I only picked it because I like to go to the movies. That's why when I say I want to make two films, what I really mean is I want to watch other people make them so I can watch them and collect the rights, royalties, or whatever for being the idea generator, the originator.

There's a store in the main office here that features demos of memorial packages. The thing is, even when they work in the business you can tell they watch to see if the reason you are "just looking" is because you are suicidal. I just know it. Especially if you're young and say you're a mother. Or maybe I'm wrong, and they're thinking, *Poor woman has cancer.* I just say I had a near-death experience in 2008 due to a twisted colon, which is true. I was told had I arrived five minutes later to the ER, it would have burst. Hence the removal of twelve inches of intestine. I don't have time to tell them about the suicidal ideation of manic depression or the slow death wish disguised as overeating.

Nor do I tell them about the other near-death experience in that banner divorce year of 2008, after a simple hernia operation. The hospital shall remain nameless. A pain medication overdose led to me passing out in the passenger seat of our car five minutes after leaving the hospital. My caring still-spouse took me back to the hospital, where we waited outside the ER while 911 was called. Due to hospital rules, of course, they couldn't just wheel me back in. Here's where the near-death experience came in, although I was told later by hospital staff I was just hallucinating. The paramedics tried to get me out of the front seat of the car, but I was busy in a tunnel of white light trying to figure out the identities of the two silhouetted figures who were inviting me to join them. When I realized it could be the end, I thought, *Oh, no, this is the tunnel they talk about.* I thought about not being with my daughters and started to yell out loud to the figures, "You can't take me!" Naturally, the paramedics thought I was resisting their rescue, and it created quite a problem. Surely that's proof of my unconscious wish to live right there, and it need never be questioned again.

The portal was so heavenly—except for the deal breaker that my daughters weren't with me—that you can imagine my disappointment when I woke up. I kept hearing someone ask, "Do you know where you are?" When I opened my eyes, all I could see was a beautiful tropical beach, so I said, "Fiji?" It turned out to be a poster on the ceiling. I guess they want to make it easier on those of us who make it back from near-death experiences. They told me I was nowhere near close to dying, which was good, and what a thrill to accidentally overdose on drugs after being a sober alcoholic for twenty years. Perhaps a normal person would have filed a lawsuit, but my addict's brain didn't even think of it. To me, it was more like a free ride without having to raise my hand at a recovery meeting as a newcomer. Not that I'd send a thank-you note.

I want to go to the office again and browse the funeral packages just for fun. I'd like to talk over my dance idea and shoot the breeze with the angels of death in the office, the death counselors. I've come a long way since I wanted my ashes scattered at sea with the J Pod of orcas in the San Juan Islands off the Washington state shore. That was before I had children. After my children told me they did not want to get in a boat around a group of killer whales to spread my ashes or even visit me there afterward, I changed my mind. Besides, I found out it's illegal to do that. It's important to check out the legality of your wishes before burdening relatives with possible jail time, lawsuits, or embarrassment, as well as exploring their comfort level with what you would want done. I'll just have to visit my J Pod while still alive.

As for existing formats and books about planning for the end, there's a reason this book may not sell well or even get published. Books like this end up on the 75-percent-off sale bin at Barnes and Noble, at best. No one wants to plan for death. But it can be fun, as I've demonstrated here.

Whatever you don't think will happen in your wildest dreams while alive, you can plan for after your death. For example, I've accepted that *forelight*, my word for pre-dawn, will never make it into Merriam-Webster's dictionary while I'm alive, so I'm having it published on my gravestone. Mom doesn't like the word; she says it's too sexual, probably because it is so close to the words *foreskin* and *foreplay* in the dictionary. That typically starts another argument between us, where I defend my position by saying, "It is sexual! Why do you think guys wake up hard in the forelight?" Anyway, the word is going on my page of the book image on our gravestone, not hers. So there. No one will be able to edit it.

Who cares about getting it in the dictionary anyway? It turns out the word was used in the 1800s by some random poet. So I didn't invent the word. But back in the nineties, dictionary editor James Lowe at Merriam-Webster said that one day I could get credit for resurrecting the word if it made it into the dictionary. I'm also adding a definition, because it isn't just pre-dawn. Forelight is an abstract concept for the single underlying principle of the universe. More on that in the *Theory of Everything* book I told you I'd write.

I used to be obsessed about what journals to leave behind until I weeded out all the words I didn't need to keep. I sought help for this obsession. "What if I can't leave the journal legacy I want to leave? What if I run out of time before I can edit, sort, and designate?" Counselor Amy replied, "You are the legacy." I have a feeling she'd also say today, "You are The Resting Place." But

I've got that one figured out now.

The only way I'm going to be able to take my journals with me is to burn them, and since I got rid of them, there isn't much left, if anything, that I wouldn't want to leave behind. So as I said earlier, I'd like to be buried with just one blank book to take me into what happens after I die.

While blank books are my favorites, another good one is a fill-in journal one daughter gave me for my last birthday. *A Mother's Legacy: Your Life Story in Your Own Words* is a family keepsake. They tell you what to write, which kind of puts a damper on "your own words." I don't really care to address things like "What would you do differently in life if you could?" What kind of question is that? Just start doing it now.

"What advice about life do you want others to remember?" Maybe if I followed advice to begin with I'd have some to pass on. But I tend to make it up and follow my own rules.

"What would you like to see happen in the next ten years?" Let me get out the crystal ball I was given a long time ago by the boyfriend before the husband. Wait, it's at home. I'll look into it and get back to you.

Otherwise, the questions are fun and memory provoking. It's best not to take it so literally that you get writer's block, feeling you have to answer the question exactly. Just write what it evokes. Think about what the question makes you think of and write that down. For example, "Describe a memorable Valentine you received." How sad that I don't recall receiving a standout. But it made me think of the sweet-sixteen card from my first love. I still have the card! And about the time I delivered seven Valentines to the mailbox of the man who would become my children's father's. At the time, I was engaged to someone else, the crystal-ball boyfriend.

Writing is a perfect legacy, as are photographs, though I'm not a visual person. Florence Littauer said, "The beauty of the written word is that it can be held close to the heart and read over and over again."

The personal planning guide offered by the office here looks like a travel magazine. And what an adventure inside. It's actually better than my *Putting Things in Order* workbook. When they handed it to me, they said, "Here's your homework." That was years ago, but now I'm ready to take the course. Now, however, I'll obsess over which book to use. Hey, they didn't tell me when my homework was due.

OMG, here's the statistic. It says that 32 percent of Americans fifty and up have prepaid some or all of their funeral or burial expenses. That's twenty-one million people. Wow, at forty-five, I'm probably in a lower percentage bracket. Did I mention I can sell this plot? That means it is an asset, too. It's in my name only. I own it. It's an investment. It doesn't make money, but it is salable. How tragic it would be to sell it after all this. It would be like selling my first home. I won't sell my first home, high in La Quinta Cove in the Palm Springs area. I intend to retire in that first home, which I bought in 1999. I received it after the divorce, and now I rent it to vacationers.

"More than ever before, people are making plans for every stage of life," the magazine says. But it doesn't say why. I imagine, speaking for myself, that all our addictions are getting worse, and we're a bunch of obsessive/compulsive control freaks.

At Gateway, I already have a real estate agent, the woman who sold me my plot, and a grief counselor, the family service counselor who assigned me my homework, the workbook. I haven't done my homework yet, but I will. I hope she doesn't die before I do it. I hope I don't die before I do it. I'll turn it in to the office for my file. When I die, family members make one call, and all the info on me is there. In case they don't have the time or energy to scramble through the 200+ journals I didn't quite organize well enough yet to not overwhelm them.

I'm so exhausted. I'm going to go home and take a nap. This was really hard work, and you see how much more I have to do to collect the artifacts and paper trail of my life, fill in the workbook, and assemble all the personal documents in one place. Then there are the creative works that will help keep me from overeating. Last, but most important of all, there's a lot of mothering ahead.

I am a resting place for my daughters. My role? To help them internalize that within themselves or reflect what is already there that they may not consciously be aware of or identify. Such a journey deserves its own motto: "Have you found your resting place?"

I want to live as long as I can to see as many of their years alive as possible. If my children's father goes first, I want to help them through his death. I'll need to help them through my mother's death, as she's the only grandparent they'll ever have known well. I want to see all the girls get married, have children, and live on their own. I want to know what they grow up to do for work and for fun. I'd like to see what our relationships are like over the years, and how they change and don't change. I want to watch myself evolve as a mother at all their ages and stages, understand how I can be a friend and mother as an adult, see how and when they choose to relate to me. I need to get better at Christmas presents, shopping for food, and staying up later at night with them. I should forget trying to cook. I'll need to help them leave home and go out on their own. I want to meet their significant others.

I don't want to die on my mother. Therefore, I must stay alive for her, as well. Also, for my children's father. I would not want him to watch his daughters go through the loss of a parent like he did. Or cause him to relive the loss of his own mother.

Time for a mother's resting place meditation, and I will report on the results.

I envisioned a book signing under the memorial tent. I called the YMCA to see if a lap lane at the pool was open. I took a long drink of water. I feel more alive than I have in my entire life. I finished the writing in five hours and will celebrate by swimming, walking, and weights. I have a shell to care for well. I'll go home, nap, eat a good dinner, tidy to tolerable, and type the first line of this book into a computer. I'll dedicate the book to my three beautiful daughters.

I cry now because I care so deeply about myself, maybe as equally as I care for them now. I am so worth living for! I have missed myself while I was dead. I can breathe now. Easily. Finally, I can rest in peace.

The Next Day

Graveside, Gateway Memorial Park

I showed up to work early today and got "paged." (Did you catch the writer's pun?) I was awakened in the middle of the night. Now I'm taking a psychotic break to tell you why.

I left my resting place less than twelve hours ago. That's how long my spirit lasted fully in my body. Until 2:00 a.m., it was a full-body experience. I left Gateway, swam laps at the Y with joy and levity, grocery shopped effortlessly and gratefully, and then poured myself into furthering the *Soul Custody* manuscript, emailing the book proposal to a publisher. Hours passed, and I even reread Judi Hollis's draft of *From Bagels to Buddha*, which will probably be in bookstores by the time you read this. I wrote her an email about how powerfully it affected me. I also told a colleague about my intention to shift Fault Line from earthquake survival plans to a one-film movie production company.

In other words, in my first attempt to leave The Resting Place with The Resting Place within me, I went places this woman has never gone before. That focus stayed with me all day. I dove into bed more satisfied, alive, at peace, and spirited than ever in my life. At last, my resting place was intact, within, permanent. I no longer felt homeless at home. I was home, and it was safe to be there.

After four hours of delicious sleep, I woke up. No big deal. Just meditate myself back to sleep. I couldn't do it lying down, so I sat on the floor in seated pose. Ah, connected. I'd be back to sleep soon. The problem was that I couldn't locate my spirit. The Resting Place had vanished. Terror struck my heart.

Then began the ritual.

When alone at night, I occasionally barricade my bedroom door with the nightstand. When I wake in the wee hours feeling unsafe even with that precaution, I lock myself in the bathroom. I sit with my back against the door and my feet against the toilet so I can brace myself if someone makes it past the first barricade. I also press the numbers 911 on my cell phone without hitting send and keep the cordless landline phone next to me. I'm ready. *For what?*

I try to meditate. If I'm lucky, I curl up in a ball and fall asleep, and the spell passes by daybreak. This morning, I was not so lucky. The spell intensified during meditation, as it came to me that my spirit was not safe. "What would make you feel safe again?" I asked. "Get me out of here," my spirit replied. I tried to talk my spirit out of it, but the demand was too strong. If I didn't mobilize, my spirit would break loose, and I'd die right there in meditation ... which is how I'd wanted to die. Because I don't want to die yet, as you and I both know, I had to appease my spirit. Where could we go at 3:00 a.m.? Denny's? I needed a resting place. Where could I find it? I couldn't go back to Gateway. Cemeteries are spooky at night, and the dead come alive and dance the way they do in *Thriller*. I felt pushed to the brink.

Because I was in meditation and calmly observant, I became quite aware that I was having a psychotic break due to terror. My spirit wouldn't come back into my body, and I was desperate. I needed to go to the hospital and check myself in. But, no, I couldn't do that. What insurance company would cover a spiritual emergency? I could call the psych ward directly and say, "Hi, I'm Pamela. I just had a psychotic break. Mind if I hang out in your lobby for a while since my insurance won't cover this?" Can you imagine it? Diagnosis: *Insane*. Thinks her spirit left her body. Room 5150, please.

Of course, I wouldn't have to tell them. If I was careful, I could make my way to the hospital chapel ... if it was open. It has served as a writing nook for me before. Redlands Community Hospital is right down the street; it takes me thirty minutes to walk there and less time to drive. I knew I couldn't voluntarily commit myself to the asylum, because I might not get out in time to pick up the girls at 10:30 a.m. Checkouts are slow, and I'd have to prove sanity, which would be very difficult or dishonest. I figured I'd go there and see how far I got. If nothing else, I'd just sit in the lobby looking like I was grieving or waiting for someone who is in the hospital. I'd get as close as I could to being safe without making myself unsafe once the word got out on me. I'd also take this book, my written resting place, with me to help the spirit return.

The biggest challenge was getting past the double barricade in my bedroom, opening three doors to get to my car, slamming that door shut as fast as possible, and locking it even faster.

Somehow, I did it. I could breathe again. I'd gotten out. Only a cop cruised the street with me at 3:00 a.m., so that felt safe. At least I had an escort.

But it wasn't over. I had a plan. Ask if the chapel is open and don't volunteer any information. If asked, say I want to pray for someone (don't say it's me). If they ask for a name, I'll say, "The person closest to me in the world (me, of course)." If they ask if the person is in the hospital, I'll say, "Not yet, but she will be." If pressed further, I'll tell them she's dying, and I need to pray for her spirit. I doubt it would go farther than that, and it's all honest.

Hospital main entrance hours don't allow me in and redirect me to the ER. Great, I'll have to step over bleeding bodies and maybe even sit amongst them just to feel safe again. I stop at the registration desk. "I'm not sick. I just wondered if the chapel is open." The code of silence kicks in. People don't ask why you need to use the hospital chapel; it's the same at the cemetery. Spiritual emergencies are never discussed. I'm in luck. I don't have to disclose a thing. I'm not asked for an ID or even my name to get beyond two sets of closed double doors. When they close behind me, it feels like the safest lockup around.

Two people scurry out of the chapel as I enter. Everyone wants to be alone in a chapel, just like at the cemetery. You're not supposed to encroach on someone's grieving space. I sign in on the "Dear God" blank notebook, on which someone has already written, "Dear God, please help my grandson Evan." I just wrote, "Dear God, help me." I hope God knows what that means, because I didn't know how to be more specific.

Ah! My resting place! At last, I can breathe, and my spirit returns instantly as I sit down. I'm wiped out from the psychotic break, my body relaxed now that my spirit is back.

Beating the system by treating my own psychotic break free of charge here in the chapel is the best deal in town. And I can still pick up the girls at 10:30 a.m., even if I have to nap all day to compensate.

My ink ran out, so I took a pen from the podium where the "Dear God" petitions go, even though the sign says, "Do not remove a pen from this podium." Really, I just switched out the empty one. Nevertheless, I feel I'm going to be busted for this infraction. I wonder if I'll even feel the need to replace the Kleenex I use.

I know what this is about; I just don't know how to get past it. All the violence from my childhood has to do with locked doors. Unsafe people opening them. People getting in. I was constantly trying to hide. No matter how much I hid, I never felt safe.

After coming out of my last food binge on August 4, I was lying half comatose in bed way before bedtime when memories I'd been trying to ward off with food started to unfurl. While this occurred in a silent but conscious state, my youngest was watching a video next to my bed and playing with stickers. She came over to place a sticker on my heart. "Here, Mommy. This is God's heart. Put it in your heart, and it will be food for you."

Here, Mommy. This is God's heart. Put it in your heart, and it will be food for you.

This is God's heart. Put it in your heart, and it will be food for you.

This daughter is a medicine woman. I felt instantly healed, fed. She must have picked up on it, because she proceeded to put heart stickers all over my PJs, feet, hands, and arms.

What a wracking dilemma. How do I convince my spirit she's safe in my shell, that I'm a safe resting place? Spirit has other evidence, too, that my shell isn't safe. I was three in New York City when an adult my parents thought they could trust entered my bedroom and molested me in the middle of the night. At the time, my shell was so small and the dark figure in my room in the night so looming, I thought I was being eaten alive by a monster who was going to get my brother next.

No wonder I've had disordered sleep my entire life. If there were nights I slept through while drunk before age twenty-two, it doesn't count, because I can't recall them. So a bed is most definitely not a resting place in the literal sense it's supposed to be. It wasn't a resting place for my spirit, and it isn't now for my shell either. Not during the time of night when the deepest, darkest secrets come out. If I stay awake, they stay in. But that keeps my spirit out.

I'm exhausted and extremely hungry. Denny's sounds really good. Is this psychotic break over yet? Can I go home now? I want a final resting place, dammit! One where I can say, "Finally!" The YMCA opens in twenty minutes. I can go for a long walk, safe under florescent lights with the early morning zombies. Part of me wants to stay here, checked in, because I'm more afraid of checking out now that my spirit is in. How do I keep her safe and not scare her off again? How do I keep my resting place? I want this book to have a happy ending, where I rest in peace, and that's it. Like when you're dead, but I'll have it while I'm alive.

Perhaps it's a good sign that I broke through the barricades at home and fled the scene.

There's the solution. The Resting Place is with me, and when it escapes me, I just have to go and get it back, as I've done this morning. No psych ward, no restraints necessary. It's better to be on my Lamictal at home than on Thorazine in a padded room. I prefer my meds to theirs, my food to theirs, my bed to theirs (except when it's unsafe), and I prefer to avoid the humiliation and shame of admitting I've had a psychotic break. We're good, because I've admitted it to myself and will call Diane, my therapist, this morning.

Go home, eat, sleep. Can I do it? What if a burglar breaks in, replicating the scenario. I don't care if someone steals; I just don't want them to come after my spirit by hurting my shell. Just because you're paranoid doesn't mean they're not out to get you.

Fear is what steals the spirit. Love is what restores it. It's that simple.

Time to leave the chapel now. Spiritual emergency treated. Cheapest hospital stay ever. The only lockup is the one I'm doing to myself at home. I even lock the cats out so they won't jump on me.

I open the door and peek out. It's safe. No one's there. No one is threatening me. I need to stop beating myself up, even over this. I do what I need to do, and sometimes that means overeating.

I'm still scared to go home, but I must risk bringing The Resting Place back home, or I'll have to spend the rest of my life at the cemetery.

Twelve Days Later

SEPTEMBER 3, 2011
Graveside, Gateway Memorial Park

I'd better write fast. I wore my Desert Queen perfume today without thinking, and I don't know whether the bees will like it. Memorial service today. Why do people wear black? The formal code should be whatever you want. That way people can ask themselves, "What would Mom like me to wear to her service?" My mom wouldn't want me in black. She'd want me in a bright floral Talbot's dress, with matching shoes and purse, the kind of clothes she always bought me. If I wore what I wanted, it would feel disrespectful. I would want her to know that I dressed her best for her.

The color of respect is not black. The color of respect is the color that brings a person self-respect. In that case, I'd better rethink the floral. The dark green wool dress I wore to her mother's service in 1989 ... now that's a living color. Hunter green. I think I will buy the outfits to wear to my parents' memorial services now. One less decision when the time comes. I hate shopping. And I'll hate it worse at a time like that.

Back to the issue of black. Once again, we have it backward.

People need to wear black for baby showers and white for death, same as the reason for grieving births and celebrating deaths.

I came back here for unexpected reasons. I need to report in on what's happened since last here. Being a person big on closings rather than openings, I need to tie together the loose ends thus far. First, the scales have tipped in favor of the living over the dying. It just happened by itself. Coming here didn't feel as exciting as before, and there was no desire for relief or experience of relief upon arrival.

Uh-oh, there are purple flowers on the living spouse side of the couple's marker! They are silk, which might indicate she did not die but is more like me. Should I leave a note? "Can I meet your son? Is he a doctor? Would you like to meet me and my mom?" But I didn't bring a baggie for the note. Now I'll have to come back here just for that.

Yes, I've come alive in my life. I took two private ballroom dance lessons and one nightclub two-step class. I'm definitely a stiff. When I told a friend who dances, I wondered if she had read my book about wanting people to dance at my service. After I told her I figured I'd better learn now so I can dance at my future wedding and anyone else's, she replied, "And don't forget dancing on graves." I was too alarmed to ask, "How did you know?"

Mom noticed early in my life that I always slept with my hands over my chest "like a princess." That's not how I see it. It's a dead-person pose, and I'm in a coffin when in that position. When I caught myself doing that recently, I intentionally turned over on my stomach and sprawled.

I saw the psychiatrist on a regular visit, and he gave me the best advice after a good checkup. "Just live your life."

I actually met some neighbors, too, not that we're pals. But I feel neighborly. I realized why I wanted to know my dead neighbors more than the living ones. You don't have to relate to them.

I wrote all week like a real writer. The dream projects have come alive.

I play dollies with my girls now, and we even got back-to-school clothes for Barbie, despite all of them violating the school dress codes.

My children's father's birthday came and went without me doing anything inappropriate. I got him a funny card featuring a cat dealing cards. It read, "Pick an age, any age." I gave him a six-pack of his favorite diet soda and a package of sugar-free breath mints, because he sings in a choir.

The Resting Place is, indeed, within whenever it's called upon. I've discovered I can stay in my resting place 24/7 if I choose. I intentionally locate it in the center of my being during each morning's meditation, and I return to it throughout the day whenever I feel I've slipped from it. Password: Just take a breath and you're in the door. It's only one thought away.

Four Months Later

JANUARY 26, 2012
At the Vet

It's inconvenient to go to the grave site right now even though I really need my resting place right now. Kiva, our Christmas Calico cat, is dying. Kiva is Native American for *ceremonial house.*

You know, I had a miscarriage twelve years ago yesterday. Pet loss brings up any and all unfinished loss, losses we can't otherwise bear. It's like the pet carries it for us, the unfinished loss. When the pet dies, it goes, too. Or not, if we block it by a million means.

Kiva is the last of the Mohicans from my marriage, adding another dimension to grieving. It's actually his cat from the marriage, a Christmas present from me to him. I made her famous in a story I wrote called "The Christmas Calico." You guessed it ... unpublished. When I saw she'd gotten worse, I stalled for an hour. Let her die/help her die? Two of my daughters predicted her death for today, when she was in better condition.

The way I view death is that it's an assimilation of her spirit back into universal love consciousness, where all spirits originate and return. She is in a body. I agree with my youngest's assessment of our other cat Nika at death: "She lost her body." She (her spirit) lost her body. But she is still alive. The love embodied in this creature disperses to the hearts of all whose lives were touched. We all get an injection of love.

I wanted to wait and see her last breath move through her. I guess I will do that if they inject her. Is there enough patience to wait for the last breath to come naturally and for free? Why pay hundreds to inject and cremate when you could wait for death and then dig a ditch for free? Our world is so orderly it's chaos.

Death brings us fully into the heart zone, where we can't fathom staying for long.

It took this to bring me to my resting place again. Notice the gap. Does the space between Sept. 3, 2011, and today, Jan. 26, 2012, even matter? It's as though nothing has happened; that space doesn't exist. It can jump as though to the next minute no matter how many calendar dates passed.

I texted my children's father a long message. He doesn't want to come, citing "Vivid memories of Io." That was his first cat, who died when we were married. He'd had her longer than any female in his life, including his mother and me. I was catching up, and then we got divorced.

I can't stay on the topic of Kiva. After this, I'll need to decide whether to pay homage to my cold stone or take a brisk walk in the park to celebrate my next breath. Today, it's okay to try to experience Kiva's transition out of her body in the way I believe for once. To not cry for others' sake.

I didn't realize the heart was the last to go. I thought breath left last. Our hearts linger the longest, eh? Her breath left. Then the barbiturate stopped Kiva's heart.

The doctor suggested putting her down, saying, "You don't want to hear her cry all night like that, do you?" Because I might lose a nights' sleep or because she would suffer? Which did he mean? My convenience or her suffering? Or, God forbid, death might linger, its tortuous length unknown. She had a low moan like a sleepy tiger or a woman in labor is all. Hardly worth losing sleep over, and what if it's all part of the process? I don't get it. Isn't she entitled to her end? Is it wrong to suffer? Should we be spared suffering at all costs? What if dying pains are like labor pains or growing pains and, for some psychic reason, we need them?

The vet said it wouldn't have been nice of me if I had opted to keep her at home writhing in the bathroom. Well, I'm sure he meant to say "humane." She could have gone days or, who knows, a week or more. I wish life were such that I could drop everything and be by her side until she died and not have to do it at 2:15 p.m. so I can pick up the girls at school at 3:00 p.m.

I could take them out of school, and we'd all be with Kiva until the end, not even worrying about it interfering with the weekend plans. Life could be *about* what we have to do, not when we have to do things. Yes, we needed to drop everything, do everything we could to make her comfortable, and wait for her to die, as long as it takes. Her time, not ours. Even if she was in pain. Missing lunch. Missing school. Missing sleep. Letting the dishes sit there. Not answering the telephone. Treating it as sacred as a birth, her transition.

Bizarre ideas come from grief. Ideas like this book.

I can't recall all that's happened. As unplanned, I started living my life. Found no need to return to the grave site yet. Decided this book itself is a resting place, so just by opening it, I'm there.

No need to leave before the gates close at sundown.

Some other day I'll fill in the gaps, maybe. Or maybe I'll just move forward, take up my resting place, and walk on.

Two Months Later

Palm Springs Convention Center, California

I'm at someone else's resting place for once. I'm the first one here for the viewing of Richard Milanovich, Agua Caliente Indian tribal chairman for twenty-eight years. Actually, his resting place will be the tribal cemetery, not far from where he was born. Security wouldn't let me into the Palm Springs Convention Center lobby half an hour early. Outside, I lit a eucalyptus mint candle. Likely, he'll be lying in a casket inside the center. There will be a four-hour service here the day after tomorrow and a tribal wake tomorrow from sundown on. I hope I'm not in the wrong place.

"Richard Milanovich represents the cultural backbone of our desert. It's what gives this area its cultural and spiritual depth." That is what I told my former employer, *The Desert Sun* newspaper. I'd best not approach anyone here but rather proceed in silence. He was big on humility. He was a substantial part of the spiritual and professional lore for me and my children's father. He liked us both as journalists, especially him. Milanovich felt

we had integrity and accurate cultural perspectives. He's another aspect of our marriage that's now dead.

Two Months Later

Home Desk, Citrus House, Redlands

I have found the ideal antithesis of the weight and depth of the cemetery gravestone as a resting place in my life: my desk. It is wooden and ornate, a small rolltop desk with ten drawers. The desk became a resting place because of that inspiring friend from the money program. We began a ritual of showing up at our desks every weekday at 9:00 a.m. to commit to our writing tasks via telephone.

The last time a desk felt like a resting place was in fifth grade at the Evan's School in La Jolla. I had stayed up all night writing an entire play, a mystery aboard a cruise ship, *The Case of the Missing Watch*. The next day, I took it in to Helen, the teacher, and she said, "I told you to come up with an idea for a play, not a play!" I was crushed. It didn't even matter that our school produced the play and I won an orange ribbon in drama. I had done it wrong. Backward! Idea first, then play. Not play and then idea. Stupid! My sense of pure, utter accomplishment gone, my desk the ultimate betrayer. Was I twelve then? I'm forty-six now and have recovered my desk. Of course, I've had no interest in plays since then, but a screenplay, yes, and five books. Five books and two movies.

I want to be an author when I grow up. So will I grow up only when I'm an author? I've wanted to be an author since as early as I can recall. The point is, I am alive, and I now have my favorite resting place in this world again, this book.

The cemetery called out of the blue the other day. "Just following up with you and seeing if we can do anything for you" type of message. I wanted to call right away and set an appointment , but I realized I don't know what to have them help me with yet. What, are they trying to hurry up my check-in? I already bought a plot, which is now paid in full. Maybe they want me to purchase the rest of the package.

Today I go for a CT scan of the abdomen, ordered due to a hernia they want to make sure isn't something else, because they think it might double as a mass in a lymph node area. Can't recall what test that was from. Oh, yeah, ultrasound. My point is if they found stage four cancer, I could avoid chemo and go straight to the grave in three months.

Consequently, I learned that one benefit of having had a death wish is not being afraid of receiving bad news. Just think of the clarity and acuity life would take on when given a deadline. People talk about it all the time.

Acuity *is the coolest word. It only has one C, which I just learned when I tried to misspell it. It means "sharpness or keenness of thought, vision, or hearing." This is opposed to clarity, which is the quality of the sharpness itself. For example, we refer to intellectual acuity. What's even better and less talked about is the concept of emotional acuity. That's far more interesting and rare. Imagine that ... emotional acuity.*

Everything unimportant is falling away. I'm becoming closer emotionally to everyone, realizing the appreciation I have for people and they have for me, seeing my life flash before me in its entirety and coming to terms with everything unfinished, like this still-unpublished journal. I'm setting up my daughters to live without me, preparing them for the end and informing them of exactly how I intend to remain with them forever. I'm creating a conscious legacy of writing and belongings to pass on and am planning my service. Perhaps I can even hold it ahead of time so I can be there for it. Maybe I'll ask the newspaper if I can write my own obituary and have them publish it so I can read it in person. Editor's note the day of the obituary: "Ms. Little is scheduled to die this month. Doctors give her until June 30."

I'll be back with my CT scan results unless I get hit by a car. Right. I'll also be back if I *do* get hit by a car.

One Month Later

"You don't have a hernia. You have a mass." Therefore, I need a biopsy. Damn. I was trying to prove a point in this book that you can have a wake-up call before it is forced by circumstance or, in this case, forced by an unknown circumstance that could go either way. Instead of receiving a wake-up call, it would be a call that you make. See the difference?

You already know the part of me that was elated after receiving this bit of information. What you don't know is that if I don't publish this book in time, I'll never get to lend my original perspective to you in the way I word it. This creates an urgency to get my five books and two movies out there before I die.

Next came the ultimate hope for a diagnosis of benign, and the number one reason is my three daughters. Let's not get all morbid before it's time. Let's focus on the doctor's phrase: "Appears harmless."

How would I act after learning it's a good result? Same as I do today, but with a little less pressure on the projects. Bad result? Same as I do today, with a little more pressure on the projects and a *hellofalotof* preparation with and for my girls, which, by the way, you know I'm already doing. You could say, then, that I did experience a wake-up call before the wake-up call, and so, indeed, I've proven the point of this book just in time.

Is the wake-up call in the potential news or in the news itself when it comes to verdicts in health conditions?

Truly, it doesn't matter, either way it goes. What matters is Love, in all directions, at all times, every day.

Six Months Later

DECEMBER 6, 2012
Home Desk, Citrus House, Redlands

I'm in that mode of "life is too hard for me." Again.

Everything about it is too painful. Interactions, situations, conditions. I need to go back to the real resting place at Gateway again, and soon.

Three Weeks Later

DECEMBER 25, 2012
Desert Home, La Quinta, California

I forgot to mention my final resting place *before* The Resting Place. That's my desert home, where I am now, where I plan to retire. It's the ultimate retreat. The quiet is so delicious you can taste the silence. The smells are soothing and stimulating simultaneously. It is the first home we purchased married, our first with our one-year-old firstborn, the home our second girl was born into, the home of my greatest spiritual awakenings, the home my last baby has been brought into, the home we once lived in married, the home I nicknamed Misión de la Mañana for its early-rising mysticism. My soul is always at rest here.

Two Months Later

FEBRUARY 17, 2013
Graveside, Gateway Memorial Park

Awww, they planted purple and yellow flowers in front of all the grave sites, including ours. My marker is still blank. I guess I'll only see it when it's blank. Or can I put my name on it now, and someone else can add the date? Or can I pick my date? Eew, what a spooky suicide clue that would be. "No one found the note. They did find the planned date; she had it etched into her gravestone."

It's too cold here at the site this morning. Forty-five degrees. I didn't dress warmly enough. It won't matter once I'm dead how cold it is. At least, I hope not. I've had a frozen spirit while alive; I wouldn't want one after death.

Today, I don't want to be *here*. In *this* life, in *this* world, in *this* experience, in *this* body. I don't like anything about it. But I love my daughters, so that's why I stay. If they weren't here, I wouldn't want or need to be here. I truly feel my function is to care for, protect, nurture, and raise them, and so I'm in this for them.

What kept me alive then in all those years before starting to have children age thirty-two?

I don't believe it's a necessity that I learn to live for myself. It just isn't a goal of mine. It isn't in my makeup or nature, and, furthermore, I don't care.

You see, discovering the forelight was such a profound spiritual experience that it makes living here look like purgatory. So maybe it isn't that I don't want to be here as much as I want to be there instead. *There* will be explained in the *Theory of Everything* book I told you about.

Suicide isn't an option for so many other practical reasons. My house isn't clean and orderly, no one else knows where my financial records are, and I haven't edited all my journals (or this book!). I'd miss California's big earthquake, my next marriage, my grandchildren, menopause, and my next meal (by the way, I'm sixteen months out of food addiction!). I wouldn't be able to see what my new website looks like. I wouldn't be able to see what my youngest child looks like as a teenager. I wouldn't be able to meet my daughters' future mates. There's just too much at stake.

Side note: How can a suicide victim be both the victim and the perpetrator of the suicide? It needs to be suicide perpetrator, not suicide victim. Duh.

I have bills to pay and computer technology to learn and a chore chart to create for the girls. My time isn't up.

I hope the people in my life won't be upset when they read this book and discover the underlying suicidal streak they never knew about. I didn't really know it well, either, until I wrote this book. It doesn't mean I don't love them or love them enough. Lots of people feel the way I do; they just don't admit it to themselves.

Even fewer can say it out loud. And when people do, some of us think, "That would be me."

I wonder what would be a good day to die? Or what calendar year? Every year, I already pass by the anniversary of the month and day of my death, the one that will eventually be etched into the marker. Unless I choose a date.

I can imagine my follow-up call to the office. "Yes, there is something you can help me with. I want to pick the date of my death; can you etch that in the stone for me in advance?" Imagine the dead silence. I almost want to do it just to find out if they've ever had such a request and if it would lead to the authorities being notified as if it were a suicide threat. In that case, the conversation could not be conducted by phone. It has to be an in-person visit so I can see the counselor's reaction.

Let's see, I'd want to die during what season? Fall? No, not my favorite. Summer? No, that *is* my favorite. Spring? Yes! Have me die on April 5. The height of my spring fever, the date over the years that has marked significant milestones of various types, personal and professional. No. April 5 is too close to my oldest daughter's birthday, which is on the 17th. Poor choice. That would always tie my death to the season of her birthday and put a downer on it for afterlife. That reminds me, I have to pick a year, too.

Obviously, this can't be decided here and now.

I'm suddenly so sleepy that I need to return to my favorite resting place today, my bed. Right now. I've been up since 2:45 a.m. I nap there every day after lunch in my pajamas. I go to bed really early when the girls are with their dad, sometimes 7:00 p.m. I never "sleep in." I do have to sleep now. Planning death is exhausting. If planning to lie down forever is exhausting, imagine how tiring is the concept of planning to wake up and walk.

In the end, there is nothing to kill myself over. It's time to give up the ghost.

One Month Later

MARCH 14, 2013
Cove Oasis Retreat, La Quinta, California

It's so far in the future. So much space in between writings. And I'm not at the grave site, again violating the basic principle and premise of this book. But I feel I must be rebellious in order to claim La Quinta as a resting place. If I don't get it in here, from here, then the ultimate resting place will be missing from this book.

This house, which I call the Cove Oasis Retreat, is listed as a vacation rental on the website airbnb.com. I had an epic spiritual experience here in the year 2000 about two years after my first daughter arrived. "Wow" is all I can say. I was looking in the mirror one night, and my blue eyes literally ignited with an ethereal glow. I saw deep into my soul as if I were not a body. It wasn't an instant; it was an experience, slowly unfolding over ten seconds. If I had to name it, I'd call it enlightenment. Yep. Definitely. No particular reason. No preceding event. No premeditated effort. It just happened. And why or for what? Who knows?

I'm one month off all psych meds for the first time in twelve years. I went off them the day after the February 17 entry you just read. I woke up that morning and gave the meds to God. Right now I'm on spring break with my daughters. I'm going to have a significant dream tonight that plugs me right back into the circuit from which I lapsed thirteen years ago, which we all know is now and never and the same. So none of this matters anyway, except to say it's the removal of the illusion that time was lost. Yes, I'm recapturing and reigniting what was going on with me then. I'm letting it unfold and happen now in the safety and security of no medicine, a higher authority, and a deep, solid trust in myself.

Fortunately, there is no one to constantly second guess me or plague me with doubts. I loved what went on here. I love what goes on here. This house is possessed by the magic of the fore-light. This house is a conduit for the universal energy of all time. It has an amazing essence of the desert, which is invisible to people.

It's time to sleep now and stop talking. Baby Buddha is coming, my youngest. She is here to be part of this mystical experience. I listen to this wise little girl. She is so magical, with an undaunted spirit that's as deep and far and wide as it gets. By the way, I could be dying of skin cancer, because of this thing on my forehead. It really doesn't matter. Life or death sentence, I'm living the way I want.

Two Days Later

I brought 99-cent white roses today. Actually, Mom gave them to me in a carload of things from La Jolla. How appropriate to bring flowers from my mother to myself at my site.

I'm not obsessed with death. I am afraid of life. Afraid of what will happen if I swim thirty minutes instead of fifteen. Afraid that being off meds now with the doctors' blessings, I'll either meet a swifter end or go back to the beginning of the book with the food. Afraid that this book will offend my relatives or embarrass my children. Afraid ... Well that's it, actually. I can't think of anything else I fear at the moment.

Wouldn't it be psycho if one day they find that meds create the fear and anxiety, thereby creating the need for meds? It's true for my antidepressant in that it creates false mania. So what if the mood stabilizer created false depression? Who cares? I'm off them. My sister asked me why. I replied, "Intuition that I don't need them anymore." That's really all.

I didn't respond right away to the inner invitation to hand them over. It took a lot of prayer and waiting. Then one day I just knew I'd had the last dose the night before. I went on them in April of 2002, when my firstborn was four. I've never been a med-free mom until now. All of motherhood has required medication. Okay, so maybe there's one more fear, that I'll turn into a scary monster. No! I have absolute faith this time, in various things. My solid Quiet Hour meditating, swimming, yoga ... and my writing. Yes, my writing. I'm going to place my faith in these things to see me through.

Any loose ends? Don't know about the skin cancer. Doctors are just leaving the wound alone for now. So many things in life are left hanging without answers or outcomes. Sorry for any disappointment regarding loose ends that I don't tie up in this book. Maybe I can answer your questions at a book signing. Perhaps the one I'm planning at Gateway for April 5, 2014. I'm getting really good at picking dates in advance now.

I had higher hopes for myself by the end of this book. I was going to put all my affairs in order. Spend years coming here, entry upon entry. But maybe books have a shelf life, like food. And this one is expiring. For the record, this is my favorite of all the books I plan to write. I have loved writing it. Someone asked me the other day what I do for fun. I thought about all the traditional "fun" things that aren't fun for me. Then it came to me. "I love to write."

What will become of my flowers if I just leave them here? Should I take the plastic off?

I applied for life insurance. They only asked about a mental diagnosis in the last ten years, and mine was twelve years ago. I still feel I won't qualify once they see that diagnosis somewhere. Who would be so stupid as to insure a person with bipolar disorder?

I applied so my children's father would have an easier time caring for the girls if something were to happen to me. He would have the girls immediately. Full time. There would be $250,000 on my policy to be used for them. It all goes to them, and yet I could name him as beneficiary, I suppose. I'll look into what that means exactly. More research! This business of dying never ends.

Who would go through my things? I have to stay alive just to supervise. And what about all my writing and the memorabilia in the garage? I have to be here to look after my stuff. Where would all that stuff go? Certainly not to his house. A storage unit? I'd better start thinking. Or start reducing clutter. My children's father loved me more than anyone, and I'd want to make this easier on him.

A cry! A cry! It's coming! He loved me more than anyone! Why does it make me cry? He loved me more than anyone. I've succeeded at crying while off meds! He loved me more than anyone! The tears flowing at my grave site while I write. That's real grief. The tears feel like living waters.

Oh, to feel feelings again. I can't describe it! How long have I been trapped in my head? What did the meds allow me to sidestep? How much did my lack of writing have to do with those meds? Here we are, words flowing like ink again almost thirty days after going off meds. Twenty-eight, to be exact.

I'm excited about the process of getting organized so it will be easy and clean and clear to vacate without a lot of effort on anyone's part. So I'll act like I died and I'm the one going through the stuff. There we go. At least I could make it nice and organized, like the journals, so they don't get overwhelmed. They'll see "Box of journals to be cremated with Mom" and "Box of journals for girls to keep." That type of thing.

I have more work to do, more research now than when I started this book. This has not been a work I've accomplished but only a topic I've opened for discussion. There was so much more to cover. But in all this time I still haven't updated the living will or done some of the other tasks I identified. I long for the sense that everything is in place now so I can die. Of course, what it really means is that everything is in its place so I can freely live now, unencumbered or burdened by baggage, excess, or disorder. I want to live cleanly, clearly, orderly, and simply.

Let's summarize:

- I have a new business to start: Soul Custody.
- *Soul Custody: Voice of the Divided Child* is ready to roll. This is one I didn't tell you about. It's a collection of daily meditations for divorced parents from the perspective of the children.
- My daughters are turning fifteen, twelve, and six. I turn forty-seven in May.
- My desert house is my real live resting place. Wow, everything has integrated into a beautiful life. This spot is even paid off! I don't see a need to use it for anything else regarding this book. Maybe I'll have a book signing here.

How pretentious. Maybe I won't have book signings at all.

This book was written graveside. I'm finished with coming here to write the book, because I've identified all the ideal resting places in my life, especially my bed, which is my favorite. So there's no need for this spot until Mom dies or I die, whichever comes first.

There's nothing to come here to figure out, nothing special

about this place over any living place. It's just a cemetery. And aside from two deaths, what else could bring me here but leaving a copy of the book on the marker as an offering. What a cool idea this was, though, to write a book from here. And it got written rather effortlessly in time suspended, as all real projects do. One day it was just over. No need to come back here.

Now I can visit all the resting places in my life. My bed, my home, my Quiet Hour, my La Quinta home, wherever I am. I can rest now, so The Resting Place is any place. The world has opened up. What was only a cemetery is now a concept that I can rest in life anywhere in any circumstances around anybody. At first it seemed as if this was the escape hatch, a place to flee to, and so I did. Gradually, places started opening up away from here.

Oh, man, I never met the doctor. Darn!

My projects don't seem that special anymore, no longer necessary or needed, essential or critical. I have them all, but I don't feel driven to complete them before my death. I was just meant to work on them until I die. I found it more important just to be with my girls in whatever ways necessary. I'm on track with them, feel current with them, updated, whatever you want to call it. Connected in the ways I'm needed. And I do it through Quiet Time and their journals, working daily to keep selfishness at bay so I can guide them and love them better.

A woman just set up a lawn chair five feet from me, and she brought a book. She's facing the wall of names I've no desire to know or tell. I have changed my attitude and now believe in leaving people alone as much as possible, saying as little as possible, and not intruding. Just being. She's staring at her mother's name. I just know it. I can sense it's her mom, but the death date is too small.

Everyone has the same idea. "I think I'll go visit the cemetery." It really is peaceful to visit the dead. There's something secure in death. It's so final. Life, on the other hand, is so insecure. Death is the great wrapper-upper. Death ties up all loose ends. Death makes it all come together in the end. Maybe there is no way to die before you die or get it all done before being done or tie up all loose ends and get everything in order before dying. It defies the nature of life to suggest dying before dying. I was just reaching for a way to live as though ready to die, and I've discovered the way by writing this book.

You see, I'm leaving my last-minute fears in these last few pages, because when I take up my pillow here today, I walk away a fearless woman. It's not life without fears. It's knowing how to release fear every time it comes up. I'm spiritually fit now. The gym membership is expiring, and I'm not renewing.

Here's how I'll use the resting places in my life:
- Bed: sleep, naps, prayer
- Desert: retreat, rejuvenation, nature infiltration
- Quiet Hour: place of the most high within, at the symbolic 4:00 a.m. hour
- Home: where I most love to be

I just realized, to the tune of bone-chilling tingles only a cemetery could generate, that there's one more place.

My body is its own resting place.

My body is a resting place for my daughter, who sits on my lap. Or an older daughter who comes for a hug or a talk. Or my youngest for a wrestle or a piggyback ride. Or a future granddaughter or grandson. My body is a resting place for others, as it is for me.

My body is the ultimate resting place! I can rest my body any-where. Ah, the moral of the story is this! What a surprise end-ing! I never would have known. The Resting Place is the human body. My soul can find rest in my own body? Think of the pos-sibilities. What does this discovery mean?

The lady left. I could sneak a peek at the date to see if I was right. When she drives off. March 30, 1941. Birth month of the woman's mom. Died last summer, so only seventy-two. Well that's not old; it must have been illness.

Back to The Resting Place being the body. So it isn't a vehicle for the soul. It's truly a place for the soul to rest. The body. A rest stop. How to be restful. Well, rest frequently. Move slowly and carefully. Drive mindfully. Don't text or call while driving. Take really good physical care of yourself. Exercise. Eat the way you know you should. Make plenty of room for prayer or meditation or contemplation. Sleep is heaven on earth. Naps are even better. Be quiet, a lot. Be still. Schedule times of nothing. Breathe.

I create The Resting Place by resting and by resting in God. So it is not a place I go, after all, or in the end. Rest is a suspend-ed way of being. Being at rest. *Sigh.* That can be done anywhere, anytime.

The sun has peeked in and shines on my white rosebush like a spotlight. I'm on my final page. Rest in peace. Unrest. The phrases cross my mind. I'm looking for one last line to finish my book but won't know what it is until I get there, and it's on the next page.

Rest is just a pause between divine activities. Rest is what sets the pace for all the projects and endeavors and relationships.

Give it a rest.

How satisfying to have produced my first body of work to share with society. I wonder how you will be affected. I'm hoping it brings you to a restful place as it did me. At best, I hope it helps treat your eating disorder and keeps you from killing yourself. I hope it causes you to think of your own body as a place of rest, so wherever you are, you find rest. You find real rest for your soul deep within. Maybe you discovered your own resting places along the way like I did. Real rest for the soul can only be found in the body. Otherwise, no matter where we go seeking rest, our bodies will betray us.

I am deeply connected to the earth. My bones are like stones underground, dislodged only during earthquakes. My breath is like the air. My blood, water. Walking above ground or existing as ashes mixed into dirt, my body is at rest. I am everywhere and nowhere, and I am not missing anything. I am The Resting Place.

One Year Later

APRIL 3, 2014
Graveside, Gateway Memorial Park

The waterfall here is especially loud today, and I wonder if it's because of yesterday's rain. Certainly, the suds in the pool where the water ends up indicate that pranksters are at it again. Today I notice how big the tree is at the edge of my plot, and I need to find out what kind it is, because it might hold symbolism for my life today.

Two spaces down, there is a blank marker like mine that I didn't notice before. Could be a pre-planner just like me. Could be anybody. I wish I knew so I could get to know the person. You can look up people's crimes, but we aren't privy to their final resting spots. I wonder why such privacy is necessary. Imagine how life would open up if we knew our cemetery neighbors in advance and met the family members of those resting nearby.

So much time has passed since I visited here in a state of mind I no longer dwell in. I thought that discovering my body to be The Resting Place would be the finale. Turns out it's only the beginning. Prepare yourself for this story. It is truly beyond the grave, the most surprising twist in the plot that I would have least expected.

After that last journal entry, I became hungrier in my life than I'd ever been. I can only liken it to spiritual starvation disguised as physical hunger. I headed into a black hole with hunger that stretched in all directions within, like a galaxy without end. The depth of my disconnection was unknown even to me at the time. Not that anything showed on the surface operation of my life. But I felt betrayed by my diary, which I thought had rescued me from the depths but instead delivered me into a greater one. Another wasted effort at a book, I decided. Curiously, none of the death streak that ran through the fabric of my being accompanied me on this descent. It had either gone dormant or been removed. I was in my body finally, and yet I felt no spirit. It was a step up from feeling not even on the planet, as well as an improvement from feeling I just wanted to be pure spirit. I was in my body at last but wanting. Wanting energy and thus seeking food.

On May 15, 2013, two months after that last journal entry, I'd had it with food. The last bite ended, and there was a fork in the road. Deep in the forelight just after midnight, I awoke to a slightly electric touch to the heart. Total alertness created a sharp, attentive "What?" The directive was "Call Marilyn." I looked at my cell clock. "No," I said aloud. "Not at 1:00 a.m." I closed my eyes, and the silent words "Call Marilyn" pushed my eyelids open wide. Well, she did say call anytime. But why her? Had she not tried to pry my hands from countless pots of coffee, stayed on the line with me while I threw out food, counseled me with her Lordy prayers that I didn't resonate with? What more is there at 1:00 a.m?

I relented and dialed the number. Out came "I have no God in my body. I believe in God, and I feel nothing, like I've been gutted. Can you help me connect with God in my body? I'll even do the Christian thing where I accept Christ if that's what it takes to put God between me and the food. I'm on my knees now; can you pray me through?"

What Christian refuses an invitation like that? Her words washed over and through me like river rapids. In an instant, I realized I didn't have to hurt or punish myself with food anymore for perceived betrayals of God by going to food instead of God. The waters dissipated, and a wave of warmth and love permeated my entire being, all at once engulfing me in an elevated state of grace and light. Entering me from its origin, and moving through my body, it then extended outward to other people. I felt love for myself and others that I didn't know was missing in my life. I loved myself and people in a deeply connected way ... all people, humankind. I felt love in all directions, for and from everyone. I knew I would never be the same again. I felt purified of my ills. I hung up the phone, and in the deep sleep that followed, darkness gave way to the most heavenly light that filled my bedroom. I had been swept up by divine love awake and asleep.

However, temptation to overeat then reached an unprecedented high. This time it felt like a diabolical force was after the love that had inhabited my body, inviting me in countless ways to snuff it out. But now I had something else to go on. The source of my resting place within, which is beyond me. It is that of the Christ body called Jesus. For the first time, I felt the link between God and people, as if the personification of God in the form of Jesus is what linked me to the human race. I was now to have a divine experience on the human level. I was to hand Jesus my food and take his other hand and walk. Suddenly, Jesus as a person and son of God made sense to me. We are all inhabitants of the Holy Spirit. God within us is alive and well. In the human body, not a disembodied spirit and not a shell. We are Spirit embodied.

While this isn't news to some, it was brand new to me. It's not like I had a Christian background that led me to this encounter. It was an out-of-the-blue divine intervention on a skeptical and cynical subject for me. And that's not all. The rest-in-God concept I'd entertained thus far became lodged in my heart. Perhaps the mind at the back of the heart, where my youngest daughter explained the mind to be located. So when I would think "rest in God" in any circumstance or situation, the heart recharged my being. It's as though the Lord corrected me, saying, "No, I am The Resting Place." There must be scripture in the Bible to that effect. And if the mind does exist at the back of my heart, I wonder if the Christ mind dwells there, as well.

This love has since done many things in my life. I shared this dark diary with family members who had no idea about the severity of my death wish. Just as I suspected would happen, I felt their love instantly as a result, and some of us shed tears together. I went back on medication for the bipolar as a nod to my brain chemistry and as a compassionate gesture toward myself. On the same day I went back on meds, the food addiction was arrested. Spiritual food took over where excess left off.

I have a ferocious life wish today that soared from the depths to the highest of heights. I am so alive. I have both feet in. I'm all in, in this life, and not just for my daughters. I have let go my obsession with death and traded it in for a passion for life. I found a new church I love, where I was the first member to be baptized just ten days ago, with my youngest daughter and me holding hands. What an upgrade, from calling The Resting Place at Gateway my church to attending a church in an old theater with other members of the human race ... people! God is such a show-off. He knew I couldn't resist an old theater venue when the church announced its opening in January of this year.

I also fell in love. No, not with Andrew Fletcher and not with a doctor. Even better, a first responder with a fire department, right up my earthquake alley. He wants the left side of my final page. I might just let him have it, because, luckily, Mom changed her mind about being buried with me. She is back to "I don't care where you put me." I did manage to get it out of her that being scattered at sea in San Diego with her husband, who died in 2003, would be an acceptable option. When my stepfather Gordon died, we accidentally threw the box of ashes in the water, not just the ashes. A seagull perched on the floating box while we laughed at our mistake, none of us ever having scattered ashes before. It took our breath away. We'll get it right for you, Mom. Unless you want the seagull, too. Let us know.

Unexpectedly, I wrote my way from the darkness to the light in this diary. The final Resting Place is here on earth. "On earth as it is in heaven." It is not in some futuristic, glorified, invisible realm. It is right here, right now. At hand. Present tense, glorified, and visible.

I am at rest in my body, and at rest in the Lord. Here it is almost Easter, the season of the resurrection and the life. The tombstone within me has been moved, and I have been freed. I am risen.

I am alive.

One Month Later

APRIL 28, 2014
Home Desk, Citrus House, Redlands

The Resting Place is up for auction to the highest bidder. I've decided to sell it, and at a higher price to make a profit, which would still be a lower price than what the same product could be purchased for today at Gateway. I need money for new paint and flooring for my home, the Citrus House in Redlands. This uprooting came about because I started thinking how unfitting the other side of the page was for my new boyfriend. He's the type who should be scattered from Mount Whitney or in the Mississippi River or in the desert. I really can't picture him confined to a page. So it got me thinking about my personality. And I'm a desert woman at heart. What am I doing burying myself in the Inland Empire on the edge of Los Angeles?

So I'll keep my cremation services, maybe upgrade from the cardboard box to a gold urn they can keep. I'll sell the plot and change my wishes to being scattered at the San Andreas fault. I'm checking into the legalities of scattering ashes inside the Coachella Valley Preserve in Thousand Palms. If they say no, the San Andreas fault is pretty big and offers plenty of other accessible places. In advance, I'll have to pinpoint a location to save relatives the trouble of finding a tour guide or geologist to point them in the right direction. I can even come up with a map once I find the spot. Yes, if the Big One doesn't happen in my lifetime, I definitely want to be at the center of the action when it hits. Why? I don't know. For some reason, I just love earthquakes. And the thought of being in the desert for all eternity is more appealing to me today than being underground at the edge of the Los Angeles smog. Family members can still visit me; they can just go visit the fault line and make earthquake jokes about my obsession with it. They just better be glad I didn't make them get into a boat.

I would then start planning and paying for the memorial services at Gateway, because there is where the ashes could be received. I wouldn't make them all hike up to the fault line for the dispersal of ashes. Only those who wanted to help scatter.

Finally, how refreshing to be able to write from home, write from anywhere, aside from my resting place. How satisfying to nurture The Resting Place within, which has been cultivated through the course of this book. How prosperous to be able to let go of the burial site, if anyone wants it.

I've rested there long enough.

ACKNOWLEDGEMENTS

Foremost, I want to thank the closest people in my life: my three parents, Mary Little, and Lew Little and Mary Ellen Corbett; my three daughters and their father; my brothers and my dear sister, Terri Roetker; godmother Phyllis Major; and the many friends who supported this book, especially my beloved, Jack Johnson.

I acknowledge the professionalism of those who helped make this book possible: literary publicist Stephanie Barko, graphic designer Jenny VanSeters, and editor Sandi Corbitt-Sears. I also want to thank business mentors Skye Kooyman and Eddie Kandela, life mentor Diane Gallinger, and longtime writing coach Bruce McAllister.

And thank you, dear readers, for being the audience I didn't know this diary would be for in the end. I'm eternally grateful for the Divine Connection which I call the Forelight, and which I believe we all share. May it guide us always.

ABOUT THE AUTHOR

Pamela Little's writing career began in the fifth grade when she won The Evans Award for Drama for a play she wrote overnight titled *The Case of the Missing Watch*. She went on to win two American Pen Women prizes for creative writing in high school. While a college student, Pamela earned recognition from the William Randolph Hearst Foundation and the Annual Hemingway Days Festival for her newspaper journalism.

Henri Raynaud Photography

As a professional, Pamela wrote the "Family Matters" column for five years at The Desert Sun in Palm Springs, managed communications for a tourism agency, attended the Betty Ford Center's Professionals in Residence program on scholarship, and worked for a Montessori school. She also received the Gannett Award for Best Enterprise Reporting and numerous accolades from the Society of Professional Journalists.

As a writing coach, Pamela helps people organize their journal collections and publish their diaries. Through her ministry, Soul Custody, she creates and conducts Marriage Memorial Services for divorced families. Pamela is currently at work on a series of daily meditation books to help parents after divorce. *The Resting Place, A Graveside Diary*, is her first book.

www.restingplaceonline.com